Eltz Castle

Ute Ritzenhofen

Eltz Castle

Großer
DKV
Kunst-
führer

DEUTSCHER KUNSTVERLAG

Frontispiece:
The oldest surviving depiction of Eltz Castle,
painted around 1663. On the right in the foreground
is Johann Jakob zu Eltz-Kempenich with the family coat of arms

Photographs by Ute Ritzenhofen
except
pages 42, 47, 48/49, 53, 57, 65, 66, 67 top, 69:
Fritz Barthel, Hamburg
pages 6, 13, 21, 39, 63 top:
Martin Jermann, F. G. Zeitz KG, Königsee
page 33: Landessammlung zur Geschichte der Fotografie
in Rheinland-Pfalz, Landesmuseum Koblenz
page 41: Geldscheinsammlung, HypoVereinsbank Munich

Translation
Kerstin Hall, Penzberg

Editorial staff
Luzie Diekmann and Edgar Endl, Deutscher Kunstverlag

Production
Edgar Endl, Deutscher Kunstverlag

Reproduction
Birgit Gric, Deutscher Kunstverlag

Printing and binding
F&W Mediencenter, Kienberg

Bibliographic information published by the Deutsche Nationalbibliothek
The Deutsche Nationalbibliothek lists this publication in the
Deutsche Nationalbibliografie; detailed bibliographic data are
available in the Internet at http://dnb.dnb.de.

3nd, revised edition
© 2015 Deutscher Kunstverlag GmbH Berlin München
Paul-Lincke-Ufer 34
D-10999 Berlin
www.deutscherkunstverlag.de

ISBN 978-3-422-02348-2

Content

A Fairy-Tale in Stone:
Eltz Castle Yesterday and Today

The road became yet steeper, and the mysterious invisibility of Burg Eltz gave us a thrill of expectation when, through the trees that closely bordered the winding way, we saw that the valley was opening before us", wrote the British travel writer Katharine Macquoid in her book "A Journey through the Eifel", "then suddenly between the interlacing branches we had a vision, a mass of pointed roofs and gables showed itself. A little farther on we came to a sign-post with an arrow pointing to a path off the road. A few paces along this path a break came in the trees, and almost without warning, Schloss Eltz lay before us. Words fail in trying to picture this castle. It is like a fairy-tale in stone; the whole scene seems to be a beautiful dream rather than anything real, and therefore any description must be poor or exaggerated." Macquoid still makes an attempt at describing her first impressions: "A wooded, cone-shaped rock rises steeply from the Eltz valley in the midst of a circle of lovely hills; crowning this rock, part and parcel of it as it seems, is a perfect maze of pointed capped tourelles and roofs, oriels, gables, quaint chimneys and dormer windows, jutting out here, there, and everywhere, till as one gazes the intricacy is almost as bewildering as it is fascinating."

Katharine Macquoid visited Eltz Castle in 1895 from Münstermaifeld, where she rented a carriage for the journey. Most visitors to the castle today follow in her tracks. They travel south through Münstermaifeld and the small village of Wierschem, park their cars in the parking lot next to the Antonius Chapel and walk the last 800 metres to Eltz Castle on foot. The first view of the castle comes as a surprise to many, as it appears below the path. The first view point offers a beautiful overview over the entire complex. In the foreground is the main gate with the main access road to the castle complex. Directly behind the gate and to the left of it are a couple of small buildings, which once housed stables and workshops. The tall residential buildings tower up behind, crowned by a maze of little turrets and chimneys. An abundance of white oriels and red and white timber-frame structures contrast picturesquely against the grey-brown stone walls and the blue-grey slate roofs. The remains of a broad wall and two towers to the right form part of the heavy fortifications.

Perhaps even more impressive is the approach from Moselkern. A narrow footpath leads from here along the small river Elz to the north. A visitor wandering along this path will see Eltz Castle from an entirely different perspective, not from above, but from one of the lowest points of the Elz valley. This is described by the narrator of the novel "Im Burgfrieden", who wanders from the Mosel to the castle on foot: "The valley narrowed. I crossed the mountain stream and followed the path along the forested mountain side – up and up. Jagged precipices wherever I looked. Above, the treetops of the forested mountains – below, the gushing waters of the Elz. Every once in a while the valley opened up, small meadows with fresh green pleasing the eye, here a clacking mill, there a lonely farmstead with grazing cattle. Then everything became increasingly gloomy and harsh, the forest solitude more solemn, the gushing of the water deeper. Suddenly I saw light ahead. I caught my first glimpse of it across a grassy slope – rising steeply between the forested hills as if reaching out for the clouds with its proud battlements: Eltz Castle, the ancient, magnificent knight's castle. It stands on a steep rocky peak, grey and withered. Unyielding walls, high gables, pointed slate roofs, rising to dizzy heights, towers, battlements and oriels, countless rows of windows – a mighty, powerful building,

Eltz Castle viewed from the valley below on the approach from the Mosel

but at the same time proud and light – the image of proud dominion."

A striking feature from this perspective is not only the surprising height of the buildings – the tallest building is ten storeys high – but also the ideal situation of the castle. Looking up from the Elz valley, one has no overview of the castle, and it becomes clear why the architects chose this location: The high rocky outcrop in the middle of the valley forms a perfect foundation. The steep precipices offer shelter. The river flowing around the rock is like a natural moat. The location is a strategic one, as the Elz valley was an important trading route, possibly from as early as Roman times, linking the trading route along the Mosel with the fertile Maifeld and the Eifel. This road could easily be controlled by Eltz Castle.

The Beginnings of the Castle

We do not know exactly when the first castle complex was built. Some believe that the Eltz family was related to the influential de Palatio family from Trier. According to this theory, the sons of Burgrave Ludwig de Palatio left Trier in 1131 in order to settle on various family-owned estates. They converted these estates into castles and changed their names to those of the villages where they lived. This would then have been the origin of the castles Eltz, Esch and Helfenstein. There is no hard evidence for this theory; however, the fact that the coats of arms of the three families show certain similarities – all show the upper half of a lion – speaks in favour of this theory.

The name "Eltz" has also been much discussed among historians. Old sources give different spellings ranging from "Elze" and "Elce" to "Elz" and Eltz". Today the names of the castle and of the river are spelled differently: the small river is the "Elz", while the family and the castle are spelled "Eltz". The origin of the word is probably Celtic. It could be the name of the grey alder, "Els" or "Else" in Old High German, which is a common tree in the Elz valley. The headwater region of the little river near Bereborn in the Eifel is also referred to as "In den Erlen" (In the Alders). The name of the river is presumably older than that of the family and it is quite likely that the inhabitants of the early castle adopted the name of their home on the Elz river – a common medieval custom. The Elz river is first mentioned in the poem "Mosella", which was written in Trier by the Roman poet Ausonius in 372 AD. One verse about the side arms of the Mosel reads: *No lesser* [than the Mosel], *the Elz flows past rich and fruitful meadows, bringing fore the country's blessings."*

The oldest surviving document mentioning a member of the family is of 1157. It is the document with which Emperor Frederick I Barbarossa presented the Trier Archbishop with the collegiate St. Maximin, the castle in Treis on the Mosel and a couple of other estates. More interesting to us, however, is the list of witnesses to this imperial gift. Among them is one "Rudolfus de Elze", the first documented resident of Eltz Castle.

This means that there must have been a castle in the Elz valley as early as the mid 12th century. This early castle would have been built during the heyday of medieval castle building. Between the 11th and the 13th century thousands of castles, the fortified residences of aristocratic families, were erected in the German speaking region alone. They usually consisted of a tower – the keep – and the living quarters – the hall range ("Palas") – and were surrounded by protecting walls. The castle of Rudolf von Eltz around 1157 would have consisted of these elements, even though there is no surviving evidence of what this complex actually looked like.

The only surviving building from this period is the seven-storeyed keep Platt-Eltz in the south west corner of the courtyard at the highest point of the rocky outcrop (fig. p. 9). It was

The late Romanesque keep Platt-Eltz is the oldest building in the castle

Eltz Castle is named after the river Elz

built on a small rocky plateau, which may explain the rather unusual name Platt-Eltz ("Platt" = plateau). The tower-like building with a square floor plan, today plastered in a sandy colour, is made out of the local greywacke and slate. A square stair tower topped with a red and white timber frame construction is attached on the east side. Two Romanesque double windows on the second floor open into the inner courtyard. They belong to the library of the Eltz family.

There is another similar mullioned window in the exterior wall of what is today referred to as the Kempenich Houses on the east side of the courtyard. It was discovered in 1978 during restoration works. Since then it is believed that this building had a Romanesque precursor.

The original cistern, the only water supply in the castle, lies only few metres from here beneath the mighty stair tower of the Kempenich Houses.

The mighty fortifications in the west of the castle also date back to this early period. Looking out over the Eltz valley from the terrace between Platt-Eltz and Rübenach House, we can see two towers and a mighty curtain wall with loopholes. It was uncovered and restored in 1976 and gives us an idea of how strong the fortifications of the castle must once have been.

Life in the Castle

The House of Eltz has an unbroken history from Rudolf von Eltz in the mid 12th century until the present time. By 1268, only four generations later, the great grandchildren of Rudolf, the brothers Elias, Wilhelm and Theoderich had split the family and divided the castle and its estates amongst one another. This was the beginning of the three main lines of the House of Eltz, who – according to their coats of arms – called themselves 'Eltz of the Golden (or Yellow) Lion', 'Eltz of the Silver (or white) Lion' and 'Eltz of the Buffalo Horns'. The latter only appears on the crest, while the coat of arms also shows the upper half of a Golden Lion.

Eltz Castle thus became a castle that was owned and inhabited by several lines of a family at the same time, a so-called "Ganerben-

A mullioned window in the façade of Kempenich House is from a Romanesque precursor of the building

Remains of the original fortifications to the west of the castle

Castle". In the Middle Ages estates were often bequeathed to a community of joint heirs, the "Ganerben", who agreed not to will their respective shares to outsiders in order to preserve the family estates. At first life was rather crowded in such a castle, but soon the families began separating the living quarters and households. They kept the same name and similar coats of arms, however, as a sign of family unity. Life in these communities was regulated by formal contracts, the so-called "Burgfriedensbriefe" (Castle Peace Deeds), which regulated even the smallest details of life in the castle. These contracts stipulated the rights and obligations of the individual inhabitants of a castle and regulated its administration and upkeep.

The earliest known "Burgfriedensbrief" in the history of Eltz Castle was agreed on 6 September 1323 between Werner, Heinrich,

Lancelot, Johann, Dietrich and Parzeval zu Eltz. The contract determines the boundaries of the "Burgfrieden" (literally: Castle Peace) – that is the area within which the contract applies – and stipulates that everyone was obliged to help and support one another within these boundaries. The mention of a parson as a landowner within the boundaries of the "Burgfrieden" indicates that Eltz Castle already had a chapel in the 14th century.

After disputes concerning property claims and legacies between the families of the Golden Lion and the Silver Lion, a new, more detailed "Burgfriedensbrief" was agreed on 15 January 1430, which gives an insight into the life and problems of the castle inhabitants. It begins with a rather general appeal for solidarity and mutual assistance: "1. The inhabitants of the castle shall not harm one another, their wives or children, nor their property,

Coat of arms of the Eltz-Kempenich line

whether at war nor during peace, but jointly protect everything living within the castle boundaries and assist one another in times of need."

Then follows a lengthy passage regulating crimes within the castle community and their punishment: "2. If someone murders someone in the castle or within the boundaries of the 'Burgfrieden', the delinquent shall be expelled from the castle and excluded from the 'Burgfrieden' immediately. He and his heirs lose all rights to Eltz Castle. They may never again enter the castle boundary, unless the closest heir of the victim declares that the murder has been vindicated." One murder is indeed documented in the history of the castle and its inhabitants: In 1372 Heinrich von Eltz from the line with the Golden Lion was murdered inside the castle by Johann von Eltz from the line with the Buffalo Horns.

Punishments for other crimes are also discussed in great detail: "3. If someone beats another so that he becomes lame he shall also be expelled from the castle and excluded from the 'Burgfrieden', never to return to the castle or its boundaries until he has undone the damages to the victim or his heirs. The elected arbitra-

tors hereof are Diederich von Monreal, Heinrich von dem Walde, who is called Brant. Should one of these arbitrators die, the inhabitants of the castle shall elect his successor within fourteen days. If they come to no agreement, the second still living arbitrator shall appoint another person and these two shall then be authorised to arbitrate within the castle boundaries. 4. If someone injures another or stabs him with a knife without killing him, the culprit shall leave the castle boundaries with his wife, child and relatives immediately and not return to the castle or be re-accepted into the 'Burgfrieden' for one year after the crime. Before returning to the castle he shall repair the damages in a form determined by the arbitrators and pay a fine of twenty 'oberländische Gulden' (Mainz currency) to the building master. This sum shall be used for the construction of the castle." The mentioned post of building master was an extremely important one. He was responsible for the maintenance and repairs of the buildings and he also organised the protection of the castle by employing guards etc.

The deed continues: "5. If someone hits another with his fist or something similar, he shall leave the castle boundary for six weeks and repay the victim according to the arbitrators' verdict. He shall further pay five 'rheinische Gulden' (Mainz currency) to the building master for building maintenance. 6. If someone swears at another person, he shall leave the castle boundaries for one month together with his wife and child."

Even the behaviour towards rear vassals and servants was regulated: "7. No one shall abuse rear vassals at Eltz Castle personally, or their property, or harm them in any way. 8. No one shall take another's servants into his services without the other's knowledge and agreement. 9. If the servants fight one another within the castle boundaries and members of the community see this, they shall separate them and either keep them or send them away. After clarification of the matter, the one who began the fight shall pay compensation and the sum of

View into the inner courtyard

five Guilders (Mainz currency) for the upkeep of the building. If the servants are dismissed, they may not return to the castle boundary until they have compensated the damages and paid their fine."

Then follow further rules for the protection of the community: "10. No one shall knowingly bring another's enemy into the castle and the boundaries within which the 'Burgfrieden' applies; if he does this unknowingly, the enemies shall immediately be removed from the castle and refused re-entry until the feud has ended. None of these enemies shall harm the person who is his enemy within one day or one night after leaving the castle. 11. No one shall harm another person, whether they are enemies or not, unless they have been absent from the castle and the castle boundaries for one day and one night. 12. No member of the castle community shall urge another to harm the body and property of his relatives, or do so himself while within the castle or the castle boundaries …"

The next paragraphs deal with guests in the castle: "13. Princes, counts and landlords, who visit the castle shall each hand a signed letter to the building master in which they declare and swear by oath that they and their entourage will adhere to the rules of the castle during their stay. A knight or a servant staying in the castle shall also declare and swear this before entry. 14. A prince, who has been granted permission to stay in the castle shall pay forty 'oberländische Gulden' (Mainz currency) sustenance to the building master before entering the castle and give the gatekeepers one Guilder. A count or gentleman shall pay twenty Guilders and a good crossbow and give the gatekeepers one Guilder, a knight or servant shall pay six Guilders and give one Guilder to the two gatekeepers. This money shall be used for the upkeep of the castle buildings." Guests were also expected to help protect and defend the castle: "15. Every prince, count or landlord shall pay for two guards; a knight or servant for only one guard. These guards shall declare and swear to adhere

to the castle rules and to guard and defend the castle like the regular guards and servants of the castle. Whoever fulfils all these requirements may enjoy his stay in the castle for up to one year."

Other regulations refer to the guarding and upkeep of the castle and determine the financing of communal building measures: "16. The members of the castle community, their heirs and descendents shall always provide money for a chaplain, pay him regularly and provide him with food. 17. They shall also pay for one guard and two gatekeepers. 18. The building master shall employ the priest, the guards and gatekeepers and ensure their payment. Johann zu Eltz shall contribute seventeen Guilders of 20 Albus to the guards' salary, the brothers Wilhelm and Lentzgen ten Guilders; the remaining money shall be used for the upkeep of the building. 19. The gatekeepers shall be remunerated together and regularly. 20. Should the building master not find a suitable priest, guard and gatekeeper, the other community members are obliged to assist him. 21. The building master should undertake repair works to the castle each year and repair the fortifications wherever necessary. Each community member shall pay two 'Kaufmannsgulden' each year as 'building and guard money'. 22. This sum shall be paid by each community member to the building master. Should he not do so, he shall leave the castle and stay at an inn in Münstermaifeld and not return until he has paid the money. 23. The year of a building master begins and ends at Christmas, the departing building master shall lay open his accounts to his successor. The building master must always be a member of the Eltz Castle community."

Finally, the deed also regulates the oath on the "Burgfriedensbrief", the possibility of writing new deeds and acceptance of new members into the "Burgfrieden": "24. Everyone living in Eltz Castle now or in future, whether they are members of the community or not, shall swear an oath on this 'Burgfrieden' for themselves and their heirs; they shall adhere to

The ruins of the early 14th-century siege castle Trutz-Eltz

this oath for evermore. In return, they shall be granted unlimited use of the castle. 25. All letters of agreement or correspondence with the collegiate in Trier or between the members of the community shall be sealed. 26. A new 'Burgfriedensbrief' shall only be written by consent of all the members of the Eltz community. 27. No one shall be admitted into the community unless he has sworn an oath on this 'Burgfrieden' and a signed and sealed let-ter has been attached to the 'Burgfriedens-brief'. 28. No one born into the community, who wishes to be accepted can be denied ac-cess if he declares his acceptance of the 'Burgfriedensbrief'.

The rules in the "Burgfriedensbrief" show that life in the castle community was by no means always peaceful. An even greater threat, however, was another conflict which climaxed in a siege of the castle in the early 14th century.

The Eltz Feud

One of the most dramatic events in the history of the castle was the so-called Eltz Feud, a confrontation between the inhabitants of Eltz Castle and a few other neighbouring castles on the one side and the powerful Archbishop of Trier and Elector Balduin of Luxemburg on the other. The latter was busy expanding his territory towards Koblenz in order to strengthen his dominion. The core of the disputes with Balduin was – and this is a typical conflict at the time – the question of the exact status of the knights of Eltz and their compeers in other castles. They considered themselves free knights of the Holy Empire, who had the right to form alliances and carry out feuds and were direct subordinates of the Emperor. The Elector of Trier, however, considered them his vassals, who were obliged to serve only him and had no right to carry out private feuds. When Eltz Castle formed a defensive alliance with the castles Waldeck, Schöneck and Ehrenburg – all of them in the Hunsrück – the elector considered this a provocation and a threat to domestic peace, and he decided to fight the rebellious knights.

Johann von Eltz was considered the initiator of this alliance and the Elector therefore focused his attack on Eltz Castle. Shying no expenses, Balduin of Luxemburg had a siege castle erected on another rocky outcrop within sight of the castle, the so-called "Trutz-Eltz" or "Balden-Eltz" (Trutz being old German for defiance). It was not only an impressive demonstration of his power; he also used this castle to cut off the supply routes from Eltz to the Maifeld. The exact duration of this phase of the conflict is not known, nor how consistent the siege was. A pile of heavy stone balls in Eltz Castle, which in medieval sieges were usually hurled at walls and bastions with catapults, indicate that there must have been some heavy fighting. Whether the castle was stormed, taken, or even starved out is not documented.

In the end it was the knights of Eltz, who asked for peace in 1333. After ending the alliance with the other three castles and renouncing their right to carry out feuds, they signed a peace agreement on 24 June 1337. Balduin of Luxemburg had won the dispute in all points: The knights of Eltz became vassals of the Elector of Trier and were granted the castle as feudal tenure.

Still today one can see traces of this siege, namely the heavy stone balls in the lower section of the inner courtyard and the bastions below Platt-Eltz, but also the ruins of Trutz- or Balden-Eltz. The latter once consisted of a rectangular, double-storeyed keep with a rampart walk and a double gate with a pointed arch. The remains of this stone edifice can be best seen from the first viewing platform on the path from the Antonius Chapel to Eltz Castle (fig. p. 15).

Stone balls from the time of the Eltz Feud

"Im Burgfrieden"

The events of the Eltz Feud also inspired the book "Im Burgfrieden", the only novel about the history of Eltz Castle. The author Anna von Bonin wrote thirteen largely historic novels around of the turn-of-the century under the pseudonym Hans Werder. Her novel about Eltz Castle elaborates the few known dates and facts about the conflict between Elector Balduin of Luxemburg and the knights of Eltz with a great deal of imagination. She describes the beginning of the siege as follows: "The messengers of the angry Bishop appeared outside the gates of the four castles, which had formed an alliance against the Archbishop and refused to give in regardless of his demands and threats, with a declaration of war. At last! The time of doubt and hesitation had finally come to an end and the pugnacious knights took to their weapons. The war began. In the same night they stormed the defence castle that was still being built on the Maifeld Hill. This attack failed, however. The Bishop's forces had wisely positioned themselves to fiend off such an attack. The fortified hill was a threatening outpost of the bishop's power far within the Eltz territory and a focal point of the battle, both dangerous and endangered. All Eltz Castle could do, was to keep its routes to Moselkern and Koblenz open, likewise the roads to the other allied castles, and to man the most important outposts until such a time when another attack should become possible."

The novel also contains dramatic scenes of siege and attacks: "The small elevated Trutzeltz was the centre of all attacks, the beginning of which announced themselves by an increase of activity in the archbishopric encampment. Soon heavy missiles began pounding the proud castle, shaking its heavy walls. Even the castle rock itself seemed to sway when hit by one of the heavy stone missiles. But the walls withheld the attacks unscathed. And the castle rock stood fast as though grazed by nothing other than a child's ball, crowned by the beautiful castle, invincible, untouchable."

The novel "Im Burgfrieden" is set in Eltz Castle

The characters in the novel are partly real, partly fictitious. In the novel Johann von Eltz – the historically documented leader of the alliance – is assisted by a certain Werner von Eltz: "'You know, Uncle Johann', said Werner, standing next to him and looking out from the tower window over the heights occupied by the enemy, 'I will never forgive the Archbishop this audacity – of catapulting Eltz Castle with heavy stone missiles. He will soon realise how futile his efforts are. But that he has the courage – God, If only I could already make him pay for it!' 'Be patient, my Werner', replied Uncle Johann. 'Just let the winter pass, then we will make Mr. Balduin pay… for his bombardment with interest. I have no doubts about it. He will get to know Eltz and its allies!'"

The siege is drawn out in the novel: "Days and weeks went by in Eltz Castle in wintry monotony. Surrounded by the enemy, shut off from the outside world, but there were no

Trutz-Eltz was erected in the early 14th century on a hill opposite Eltz Castle

more attacks or bombardments. There was an unspoken ceasefire and the only indication of war was the alerted state of the troops in the castle by day and by night. The different knightly families living in the castle spent the long evenings assembled by a warming fire in cheerfully lit rooms to talk and while away their time, the men drinking from tankards, the women sitting at their spinning wheels. Often it was at Johann's hospitable table in the large hall of the Platteltz, where they enjoyed their evenings."

Following a second unsuccessful attack, the Trier Elector changed his strategy: "The attack on the proud castle was not repeated. It was too obviously invincible, the losses on the side of the besiegers were too great and did not lead to the desired success. Archbishop Balduin was quite knowledgeable in matters of warfare, having gained considerable experience during his journeys in Italy with Emperor Henry, his brother. He employed this here. No futile repe-

tition of the attack – permanent siege – starving out – that was to be his plan of war."

In the novel, following a successful sortie, the events then culminate in an open battle between the knights of Eltz and the Elector's army near Pyrmont Castle: "At the end of the long summer's day, when the sun had disappeared blood-red behind the hills, the opposition of the Bishop's forces was finally broken. The last attack had failed and the enemy troops dispersed in a wild flight." Such is the re-interpretation of the peace agreement and the end of the siege as a defeat of Balduin and a victory of the Eltz knights.

The novel "Im Burgfrieden" thus has a happy end with festivities on Eltz Castle that lasted for several days, a double wedding in the castle chapel and the consecration of a new altar: "The court was decorated with garlands and colourful flags. Pots with pitch stood near the entrances and in corners, ready to be lit in the evening to light up the magnificent space. The

View of the towering Kempenich and Rodendorf Houses with the coach house in the foreground

musicians and jesters waited in the goldsmith's house in the forecourt … the little bell in the castle chapel chimed happily, and the expectant crowds arrived in their festive gowns. The scent of roses and lilies filled the sacred space, glowing light fell through the stained glass windows. Mr. Arnold zu Eltz, the Bishop of Kamin, consecrated the new altar with the holy relics, the Archbishop's peace gifts … the bell rang and praised the Lord. The festivities had come

to an end. And so had the Eltz Feud, this great event in the history of the castle and its proud lords. Victory and Peace held their glowing halos over the venerable walls, casting them in the majestic light of good fortune and grandeur that has lasted until the present day."

The Enlargement of the Castle

A long phase of intense construction work began on Eltz Castle about one century after the Eltz Feud. After Klein-Rodendorfer House, that was already built around 1300, the three main family lines erected their own separate hall ranges: The line Eltz of the Silver Lion made the start with the Rübenach House, followed by the line with the Buffalo Horns with the Groß-Rodendorfer House and finally the line with the Golden Lion with the Kempenich Houses.

The late Gothic Rübenach House was built in the 1440s on the westside of the inner courtyard. The name of the building goes back to the family estates in Rübenach near Koblenz, which the line of the Silver Lion already had acquired in the early 13th century. It is not known exactly when the foundation block was laid, but investigations of the building materials prove that parts of the house originate from 1441/42 and others from 1444. The building has eight storeys and a rectangular floor plan. It has a striking façade, as only the upper floors are plastered and painted white. The top floor is slightly wider than the lower part of the building, projecting out above a frieze of small round arches. The turrets in the corners have different shapes: those facing the valley are round and plastered, while those facing the courtyard are timber-frame constructions. The steep roof is interrupted in the centre by large dormers decked with slate. When looking at Rübenach House from the Eltz valley, one can see a small red and white timber-frame corbelled oriel, a medieval latrine. The wall facing

The outer façade of Rübenach House

The chapel oriel on Rübenach House

Timber-frame oriels on the outer façade of Groß-Rodendorf House

the inner courtyard is dominated by two an- nexes. Above the entrance with its rounded arch is a square, white oriel with a tripartite window, which is supported by two round basalt columns. Most prominent is the late Gothic chapel oriel on the first floor of the building which was attached at a later date. It rests on consoles and is beautifully decorated with narrow pointed windows and elaborate tracery.

The construction of the Groß-Rodendorfer House began in 1515 along the northeast flank of the inner courtyard, right in-between the Rübenach House and the already existing Klein-Rodendorfer House. The name Roden- dorf, too, refers to external estates owned by the Eltz family, in this instance the dominion of Rodendorf in Lorraine. With its ten storeys and a height of more than forty metres, the Groß- Rodendorfer House is the largest building in the entire castle. Its façade is slightly darker than that of Rübenach House. The three red and white timber-frame oriels crowning the façade of Groß-Rodendorfer House can be seen beautifully from the approach to the main gate. For storeys below is another white oriel with three windows framed with tuff, which dominates the lower parts of the outer wall. The wall facing the inner courtyard is crowned by another red and white timber-frame oriel. The entrance to the house lies beneath an ele- gant Renaissance structure and a steep roof. The small mosaic depicting a Madonna to the left of this structure dates from the 19th century.

Finally, in the 17th century the third line of the Eltz familiy built the Kempenich Houses on the southeast flank of the inner courtyard. Like the Rübenach and Rodendorf Houses, the name of this building, too, refers to estates owned by the family, in this instance the dominion of Kempenich in the district of Adenau. The most recent part of the castle complex was erected in several phases – which are occasionally cor- related with the sections Groß-Kempenich, Klein-Kempenich and Burgthorn. The labyrin- thic building has only one entrance, namely a door on the left side of the upper part of the inner courtyard, where nowadays visitors ring the bell for a guided tour. It is sheltered by a narrow gate hall beneath a small oriel, plastered white and resting on basalt pillars. The round arches connecting these octagonal pillars bear an inscription with the names *Borgtorn-Eltz*, and *Eltz-Mercy* as well as the year *1604*, which commemorates the beginning of the construction of the last part of the building. The date *1651*, which is visible on one of the keystones of the small vault in the gate hall, refers to the final completion of the Kempenich Houses under Johann Jakob zu Eltz. The façade of the house is dominated on the courtyard side by a mighty, plastered stair tower, which is crowned by a red and white timber-frame construction. The exterior wall facing towards the valley is kept very plain, structured only by two red and white timber-frame oriels.

The roof landscape

The entrance to Kempenich House

With the Rodendorfer and the Kempenich Houses the whole castle complex was complete. The picturesque complex grouped around an inner courtyard and consisting of tall keeps nestling closely against one another was built over a period of more than five hundred years. Even though the various buildings reflect different architechtural styles – ranging from Romanesque to Baroque –, the complex as a whole forms a diversified, but extremely harmonious ensemble at the same time.

To many this quaint, labyrinthic building appears like a fairy-tale castle. "The confusion of steep roofs and turrets is like ancient ruins or old pictures and engravings come to life", is how the art historian Georg Dehio characterised Eltz Castle in his famous compendium about German monuments, *Handbuch der deutschen Kunstdenkmäler*. "Its solitude and the beauty of its location stimulate the imagination and make it the 'castle par excellence'".

The Family History

The House of Eltz gained power and importance far beyond the direct vicinity of the castle, possessing estates in Koblenz, Boppart, Trier, Mainz and Eltville. Many family members became known for their positions in the church, the military and in politics. As early as 1300, one of the family members, Arnold zu Eltz, even became Bishop of Kamin in Pomerania.

Most family activities focused on the two electorates Trier and Mainz, however. Two centuries after the dispute between the knights of Eltz and Elector Balduin of Trier in the Eltz Feud, Jakob II, another member of the Eltz family, was made Archbishop and Elector of Trier. Jakob was born in 1510 in Eltz Castle as the son of Johann zu Eltz and his wife Maria von Breitbach. He studied law and theology in Heidelberg, Louvain and Freiburg, before becoming canon of the cathedral in Trier in 1535 – a member of the cathedral clergy – and thus entering into a long career with the clergy. In 1547 Jakob became dean (vicarius capitularis) of Trier Cathedral, an important administra-tion post in the electorate of Trier. He took holy orders in 1550 and expressed himself at the Diet in Regensburg and the Religious Talks in Worms as an avid opponent of the Reformation. Jakob also became actively involved in fighting the first reformation movements in Trier in the 1550s – a fact which inspired a later church historian to characterise him as "the embodiment of the spirit of the Counterreformation". Even as the principal of the University of Trier Jakob actively propagated the Catholic cause and began working together with the Jesuits. After his appointment as Elector in 1567 he never deviated from his principles and dedicated his efforts to preserving Catholicism in the electorate of Trier. This was not always easy, as Lutherans and Calvinists were becoming increasingly influential. At one time Jakob even had to govern the electorate from the vicinity of Wittlich and enforce his return to Trier in tenacious negotiations and finally even by force of arms. After his return to Trier the town swore an oath of loyalty and obedience to him on 27 May 1580. Jakob died only one year after this victory at the age of 71 and was buried in Trier Cathedral.

Jakob III zu Eltz, Elector and Archbishop of Trier from 1567 to 1581

Philipp Karl zu Eltz, Elector and Archbishop of Mainz from 1732 to 1743

This engraving shows the signing of the Peace of Westphalia, which was attended by Hugo Friedrich zu Eltz as the envoy of the Elector of Trier

Another important figure in the history of the electorate of Trier was Johann Jakob zu Eltz – the same man, who also played an important role in the construction of the Kempenich Houses. The elector of Trier appointed him "Erbmarschall" in 1624, thus putting him in charge of military matters. Another member of the Eltz family appeared on the horizon shortly after the death of Johann Jakob, who belonged to the line Eltz of the Golden Lion: Hugo Friedrich from the line Eltz zu Bliescastel and Rodendorf was the Trier envoy at the Westphalian Peace conference in Münster at the end of the Thirty Years War.

In the 17th century, when a number of wars destroyed countless German cities and castles, members of the Eltz family proved to be clever diplomats. The fact that Eltz Castle was not affected by the Thirty Years War, for example, is owed to the politics of the Eltz-Bliescastel-Brunswick line, the only Protestant line of the Eltz family. The diplomatic efforts of Hans Anton von Eltz-Üttingen were also most successful. As a French officer during the Palatinate War of Succession from 1688 to 1689, when nearly all the castles along the Rhine and the Mosel were destroyed by the French, he managed to save Eltz Castle.

While the 16th century saw a member of the Eltz family become an influential Archbishop and Elector of Trier, another family member became Archbishop and Elector of Mainz in the 18th century. Philipp Karl was born as the son of Johann Jakob zu Eltz-Kempenich and Maria Antonetta Schenkin von Schmittburg on 26 October 1665. He was the second of 17 children. Perhaps it was an omen that one of his godfathers was Johann Philipp von Schönborn

– then Elector of Mainz – and another Karl Kaspar von der Leyden – then Elector of Trier – a fact which shows how well-connected the family was. At the age of ten Philipp Karl was sent to a Jesuit school in Koblenz. He entered the German-Hungarian College in Rome in 1686, which he left two years later after his ordination. His clerical career was a typical one: first canon in Mainz and Trier, then cathedral choirmaster in Mainz and dean of the cathedral in Trier. Philipp Karl was also politically active, however, for example when he represented the imperial interests of Charles VI during the election of Georg von Schönborn as Elector of Trier.

After the death of the Mainz Elector Franz Ludwig von Pfalz-Neuburg, Philipp Karl was unanimously elected his successor by the Mainz cathedral chapter in 1732. When he heard of the chapter's intentions, Philipp is said to have been rather hesitant at first, as he was already 66 years old and had no longer expected to hold such an important post. He gave in to the chapter's wishes by accepting the election and was consecrated by Elector Franz Georg of Trier in the cathedral of Mainz on 18 November. As archbishop and elector of Mainz Philipp Karl was also "Reichserzkanzler" (the highest post in the Empire after the Emperor) and thus the most influential cleric north of the Alps. He came next after the Pope himself. His election was viewed positively by the Vienna court and the relationship with Emperor Charles VI was to remain a good one for a number of years.

One year after the election of Philipp Karl Emperor Charles VI awarded the title of count to the family Eltz of the Golden Lion. This honour was owed to the family's services rendered during the Reformation and the Turkish Wars, but most certainly also to Philipp Karl's achievements, namely his engagement in the Polish War of Succession, a power dispute between the Houses of Habsburg and Bourbon in which Philipp Karl supported the Habsburg side. In addition, the family was also given the privilege to ennoble people in the name of the

Emperor, appoint notaries, scribes and judges, liberate serfs, legitimise illegitimate children and award non-aristocratic coats of arms with shields and crests.

Emperor Charles VI also thanked Philipp Karl by recommending him for the dominion of Vukovar in the Croatian part of Slovania. This enormous estate near Belgrade had previously belonged to the Count of Kuffstein, who now gave in to the Emperor's plea and sold it to Philipp Karl zu Eltz for 175 000 Rhenish Guilders. One generation later the Eltz-Kempenich line moved its main residence to Vukovar and lived there until their expulsion in 1944.

When succession disputes arose after the Emperor's death, Philipp Karl was forced to make one of the most difficult decisions in his life. Even though his sympathies lay with the House of Habsburg and he would have liked to vote in favour of Charles VI's daughter Maria Theresia at the election for the new emperor, the political situation – namely the interests of the electorate of Mainz and pressure by Bavaria – forced him to vote for the Wittelsbach Karl Albrecht. The election took place in Frankfurt at a time when Karl Albrecht, the future Emperor Charles VII, resided in Mannheim, where he received notification of his election. The conveyor of this important message was Anselm Casimir zu Eltz, the nephew of Philipp Karl.

Philipp Karl died in the year following the imperial election aged 78. Before his death he had commissioned his tomb out of red and black marble, which is still in Mainz Cathedral today. His heir was his nephew Anselm Casimir; parts of his extensive library, however, were bequeathed to the University of Mainz.

Anselm Casimir zu Eltz-Kempenich was born in 1709 in Koblenz – an indication that Eltz Castle was no longer the family's main residence at this time. In 1738 he married Anna Johanna Eva Josepha Baroness Faust von Stromberg, the last member of the Faust von Stromberg family. In order to preserve the name of her family, Anselm Casimir added the title "genannt (called) Faust von Stromberg" to

The genealogical table in the treasure vault was commissioned around 1663 by Johann Jakob zu Eltz-Kempenich (oil painting)

the name Eltz-Kempenich. This tradition is still adhered to today.

Anselm Casimir's son Hugo Philipp zu Eltz-Kempenich, who was born in 1742 in Mainz, also led an interesting life. He was the first member of the Eltz family to personally travel to Vukovar in order to visit the estates, the family's most important property that had been acquired by Elector Philipp Karl. Hugo Philipp witnessed the occupation of the Rhineland by the French during the Napoleonic Wars. As the French authorities assumed that he had fled like so many other noblemen, his property – including Eltz Castle – was seized and placed under command of the French garrison in Koblenz. Some of the Eltz estates suffered greatly under the French occupation, and the caretaker of Eltz Castle, too, had to supply the French troops with firewood from the sur-

rounding forests. The castle itself remained undamaged, however. When the French discovered in 1797 that Hugo Philipp had not emigrated, but had stayed in Mainz, they returned his property.

Even though his main residence was in Mainz, Hugo Philipp and his family were still much attached to the castle. In 1815 he was able to buy the section owned by the Eltz-Rübenach line, which included not only Rübenach House and some land, but also the Platt-Eltz. Hugo Philipp paid 3000 Guilders for this property. The Eltz-Rodendorf House had already passed into the hands of the Eltz-Kempenich line after the decline of the Rodendorf line, and the Eltz-Rübenach line had not lived in the castle for some time. This last acquisition made Hugo Philipp the sole owner of Eltz Castle. He died in Koblenz in 1818 and was buried according to his wish in the family vault beneath the chapel of Eltz Castle.

Hugo Philipp's eldest son Emmerich Josef, born in Mainz in 1765, was the first family member to move his main residence to Vukovar. He cannot have spent much time there, however, as he was ambassador to the Emperor and travelled to many different countries, spent some time at the Spanish court and later lived in Brazil after having been asked by the Emperor to accompany the Austrian Princess Leopoldine to her marriage with the Crown Prince of Portugal and Brazil. Emmerich Josef and his wife Marie Henriette were the first members of the family to be buried in the family vault in Vukovar.

As Emmerich Josef's sons both died young, his estate passed to his brother Jakob. "Count Jakob enjoyed frequent stays in the ancestral seat Eltz" wrote the historian of the Eltz family, Friedrich Wilhelm Roth, "just as he cared for the improvement of the buildings. In 1838 he spent 461 Thalers 11 silver Groschen and 6 Pfennig, and in 1839 another 427 Thalers 21 silver Groschen and 11 Pfennig on repairs to Eltz Castle."

Restoration and Romanticism

The exceptional condition of Eltz Castle today is largely owed to Jakob's son Karl zu Eltz, however, the present owner's great-great grandfather. He inherited the castle in 1844 and spared no efforts during the following decades to preserve and restore the buildings: "Count Karl made it his task to care for the ancestral Eltz Castle", reports Friedrich Wilhelm Roth, "[He] had the sections Platt-Eltz and Rübenach House as well as the chapel restored and all the interiors refurbished. While there had always been two employees living in the castle and it was in a fairly good state of repair, the sections bought from the Eltz-Rübenach line lacked sturdy roofs … The restoration began in 1845

under strictest adherence to the ancient details." The last sentence is important, as it shows that Eltz Castle was not restored in the typical 19th-century manner with great imagination and only vaguely reminiscent of the medieval style, but that the conservation of the existing buildings and elements was the prime concern. The restoration works lasted until 1888 and cost 184000 Marks – an enormous sum of money at that time, which would be the equivalent of eight million Euros today.

The painter Eduard Knackfuß was commissioned by Count Karl with the restoration of the murals inside the castle. The artist wrote about his particular attachment to Eltz Castle in his memoirs: "My father had been 'Oberrentmeister' (chief administrator) under Count Karl zu Eltz for some time and had his offices in Eltz Castle. Thus this gem of medieval Romanticism caught my attention and was henceforth to play an important role in my life. Parts of the extensive building with its large number of rooms were rather dilapidated at the time, because no one lived there. They would have fallen into complete decay, had not Count Karl decided to restore the castle with all its buildings and furnish it appropriately. The decorative murals gave me an opportunity to work on this project, as my father recommended me to the Count." Knackfuß therefore spent some time in Eltz Castle during the early 1880s. He supervised the restoration of the colourful murals in the bedroom of Rübenach House, designed the decoration of the small study in the same building and painted the family coats of arms on the walls of the great hall in Groß-Rodendorf House.

As Karl Count zu Eltz was extremely interested in the history of his family, he also commissioned a family history. In July 1888 he employed the Wiesbaden historian Friedrich Wilhelm Roth, who spent the following months in a number of archives in Trier, Koblenz and elsewhere, studying documents about the Eltz family in Eltz Palace in Eltville as well as in Eltz Castle and even travelling as far as Vukovar. The result of his research is a comprehensive

William Clarkson Stanfield, Eltz Castle, around 1830

two-volumed "History of the Lords and Counts of Eltz", which was published in Mainz. The first volume was published in 1889, the second in 1890. Roth assembled a large number of dates and facts about all the known family members since Rudolf. There are also genealogies, portraits, period photographs of the castle as well as of the tombstones of important family members.

Eltz Castle was discovered as a site of interest among travellers as early as the 19th century. Its most prominent guests include celebrities such as the author of "Der Struwwelpeter" (Shock-headed Peter), Heinrich Hoffmann, and the French author Victor Hugo. The latter visited the castle on 28 August 1863 together with two friends. Approaching from Karden on the Mosel, he jotted down his impressions in his diary, which was later published under the title "Choses vue": "Rented a carriage to travel to Elz [sic]. Left for Elz Castle at two o'clock … At a farmhouse continued on foot … Down the hill into a thick wood. Our Prussian [= the driver] followed us. He showed us the way. A winding path through the thicket, already covered by a layer of dry leaves. Half an hours' walk through the forest.

Suddenly a little river, a bridge like an elongated rack wagon wedged from bank to bank. This bridge ends in a wooden stair with six steps, slightly wet from the current. We raise our eyes. The castle appears through this clearing, like a huge window in the forest. High, mighty, surprising, sombre. I have never seen anything like it. One could describe it as an accumulation of high gables, hastily grouped around a peak. Small belfries, open arbours, latticed windows, lanterns, machicolations, watchtowers, window niches with oriels. Steep rocks. Here and there around the rocks groups of towers leaning against the castle to defend the access road. Here and there gates with portcullises spanned by pointed arches, worn, slippery basalt stairs. We climb up.

We reach a narrow platform with a parapet above the precipice. After a few broken steps a gate made of raw oak with an iron knocker, as large as the tongue of a church bell. Our guide knocks. The only answer is furious barking. The castle seems angry and transforms itself into an enormous barking hound before our eyes. No human sound. We knock. The dog barks. No one there.

Charles and Busquet go exploring. I stay alone and sketch a tower. Half an hour goes by. A man comes with a dog and a gun, then a woman. The man looks me over, the dog sniffs me, the woman watches me, the gun remains silent. Everything is ancient. I communicate with sign language. They fetch the key. Charles and Busquet return. The man goes away. The woman opens the gate. We enter.

The stair continues. A flap like in a prison. We pass a second gate. It leads into a narrow courtyard. Extraordinary. Towers and gables as far as the eye can see. 12th-century heaviness, 16th-century refinement. Windows with huge iron bars, others with fine Renaissance lattice-work. The apse of a Gothic chapel with stained glass windows. At the far end a dilapidated square tower. Two chained dogs howling at one another. Five or six sea eagles nailed to the opposite wall.

The interior: first a hall from the period of Luis XIII. … Then a number of Gothic rooms, canopy beds, beautiful tapestries, mirrors, cabinets-on-stands, weapons, a bed with beautiful woodcarvings. A chandelier made out of antlers with ten points, a golden mermaid with the Elz coat of arms on her stomach rising up in the centre. A Luis XIV mirror and sideboard, inlays and gold of unexpected beauty. Everything is whitewashed. Poverty and splendour. We see only one tenth of the castle."

Visiting Eltz Castle in the 19th century was a most difficult undertaking that had to be carefully prepared. First one had to send a written application to the owner of the castle. The Baedeker for the Rhineland, for example, described visiting regulations for Eltz Castle as follows: "The courtyard is always open to the public, the interior, however, which has been restored in beautiful simplicity, is only open

The oldest photograph of Eltz Castle was taken in 1886 by the English photographer Joseph Cundall

BURG ELTZ, RITTERSAAL.

BURG ELTZ EINGANG.

BURG ELTZ, WESTSEITE.

Gruss von der Burg ELTZ.

BURG ELTZ HOF.

B 718. Kunstanstalt Lautz & Isenbeck Darmstadt.

Historic postcard of Eltz Castle

during the week by special permission of Count Eltz in Eltville, application for which must be submitted in writing one week earlier." There was also no proper road leading to the castle. The journey via Moselkern still sounds rather adventurous in the Baedeker of 1895: "The road from Moselkern to Eltz ($1^1/_2$ – 2 hours) passes directly through the stream on numerous occasions. Visitors on foot follow the same road, past the church or underneath the railway line, climbing along the left bank of the Elz river for about 25 min. The path continues to the left behind the mill along a garden fence, up the steps over the Mühlgraben and at the bend of the slope, after approx. 5 min, back onto the road, then on another footpath, over a footbridge crossing to the left bank and up to the castle." A considerable number of visitors must have visited the castle in spite of this complicated route description, because some tourist infrastructure had developed in the vicinity of the castle by this time. The same Baedeker, for example, contains the following practical recommendation: "Refreshments obtainable from the forester below the castle."

British Travellers

British travellers played an important role in making Eltz Castle a popular tourist destination. They began travelling to the Rhine and the Mosel as early as the 19th century, seeking the picturesque landscapes – abundant with castles and ruins – that confirmed their Romantic notions of Germany. As soon as the ban on continental travel was lifted in 1815 after the end of the Napoleonic Wars, the British flocked to the Rhine and the Mosel in droves. Eltz Castle was one of the sites favoured by early British tourists and is even mentioned in English travel guides at the time, for example in "A.W. Schreiber's Guide down the Rhine", which was published in London in 1818. Some pages of a guestbook begun in 1840, which also mentions where castle visitors came from, contain more English than German entries. It is, therefore, hardly surprising that English painters and writers began visiting Eltz Castle, too. The English landscape painter William Clarkson Stanfield, for example, visited the Rhine and its subsidiaries several times between the 1820s and 1860s and also made sketches of Eltz Castle (fig. p. 31).

William Turner was deeply impressed by the castle. He visited Eltz Castle several times during his extensive journeys along the Rhine, producing an entire series of sketches and watercolours. The famous painter from England visited Eltz Castle for the first time in 1840. He had prepared the journey carefully and even copied the passage about Eltz Castle from the Traveller's Guide down the Rhine into his diary. At his first visit Turner only sketched the castle from the viewpoint near Trutz-Eltz, about the same view Stanfield had chosen a couple of years before. When he returned to the Elz valley one year later he spent more time there. This time he wandered down into the valley

William Turner, Eltz Castle from the East, around 1841

William Turner, Eltz Castle, around 1840

and circled the entire rock in order to sketch the castle from different angles. Entries in the guestbook show that William Turner must have visited the interior on a number of occasions.

English visitors produced not only a large number of paintings and sketches of Eltz Castle during the 19th century, but also the oldest known photograph of the castle (fig. p. 33). The London photographer Joseph Cundall was travelling through the Rhineland together with the architect and graphic artist John P. Seddon, when he took this photograph. The two men were documenting the historic buildings in the region for the Architectural Photographic Society, a London organisation specialised in architectural photography. They took 22 photographs for the photographic archive of the Architectural Photographic Society. A selection of these photographs – including that of Eltz Castle – was published two years later in Seddon's travel report "Rambles in the Rhine Provinces". This was quite a novelty, as similar German publications, travel guides and reports, about the Rhine and the Mosel were – at best – illustrated only with lithographs, engravings or woodcuts. Seddon describes the adventurous conditions under which he took the first photograph of Eltz castle: "But though the way was long and steep, the time occupied in this preliminary operation was comparatively short, for the scent of a photographer for the available points of view is as keen as that of the eagle for his prey, and it was evident at a glance that there would be but small choice in the matter. Yet the hunt was sharp while it lasted, for though the decision was universal that it must be from nearly opposite the entrance to the castle, the question of the level was important, and that of the road itself appeared to be considerably too low. So, like a pack of hounds, we rushed into the brushwood and over the rocks at once, first one giving tongue and raising a view-halloo that from this crag it stood out charmingly, then another vaunting that his stand-point must be a better one, and all for once seeming to neglect the considerations as to whether the camera could be, by any possibility, hoisted to where he had himself just managed to clamber up like an ibex. At last the position was secured from which the accompanying view was taken, about twenty feet above the road, as giving admirably an idea of the depth of the ravine bridged over the entrance passage to the castle, as well as of the stupendous height of the building itself. It certainly did not appear to be a very secure spot for the operation, and the scramble up to it by the help of some friendly bushes would evidently be a rather difficult one when laden with the plates for exposure; but to photograph Schloss Elz we had come, and no difficulties should daunt us from doing it in the best manner practicable." The adventurous men from England transported not only the large, heavy camera and the plates for the photographs, but also an entire tent with a fully equipped darkroom and all the required chemicals to Eltz Castle. This could hardly be avoided in the pioneering days of photography, as the glass plates for the photographs could only be made light sensitive in a darkroom immediately before the photograph was taken. It was also common practice in those days to develop the images immediately in order to check whether the quality was good enough. Seddon continues: "Soon the camera was in place, and the legs of the stand were pushed with unusual force into the soil, and before long two negatives were successfully obtained. Good generals, however, should never be caught unawares, and our experience of German weather had been so great that we ought to have expected that six hours' sunshine would be followed by a storm; but the quiet beauty of the scene had quite lulled all such fears, and some of us had strolled within the outer castle gates, and others to the brink

of the plashing Elz below, when a sudden gust aroused our operator's attention, and he looked upwards from the tent where he was working to the crag on which the camera had been standing, just in time to see it lifted bodily into the air, and, turning a somersault, come crashing, lens downwards, into the middle of the road below: running forward in the hope of saving it, the whirlwind blast swept off its legs the tent that he had left behind, and in which he had placed the last negative that had been taken. Rueful, as may be imagined, were the glances of the hastily assembled party at the *débris* of their *materiél* which greeted them. Of course, no one expected a fragment of either camera or negative to remain fit for use; but, wonderful to relate, the tent was picked up with the glass negative within it absolutely uninjured, the delicate film of collodion not being even scratched, and from this very plate our illustration is given."

What a visit to the castle was like in the 19th century is described in detail by the English travel writer Katharine Macquoid, who visited Eltz Castle at the end of the summer in 1895. She avoided the difficult route from Moselkern by renting a carriage and driver in Münstermaifeld, which took her to the Antonius Chapel. The last part of the journey was covered on foot. Katharine Macquoid describes this visit as a unique experience and portrays the atmosphere of the castle as almost magical:

"From where we stood we could see our narrow road winding steeply down to the bridge which spans the river, and then passing through a roofed archway the path rises to the higher level of the castle platform. We followed this road, feeling that we were on our way to an enchanted castle, and, if we found entrance, might possibly come forth from it bewitched, transformed, perhaps into the red and blue winged grasshoppers that flitted in great numbers across our path, spots of colour alighting here and there, as if they enjoyed the burning sunshine. It seemed truly magic ground.

Even when we were close to the Schloss its foundations appeared to be incorporated in the rock itself; parts of the building looked as if they were carved out of the dark stone. We went up some steps in the rock and then through a wonderful series of steep, winding ways and entrances, before we finally gained the inner Hof or courtyard on which the principal door opens. All was silent and deserted; no swarthy maidens or fierce lions had barred our way, though the courtyard in which we now stood seemed to be in the heart of the building, which frowned upon it on all sides.

As we pulled the bell, we saw written over the doorway, 'Burghaus-Eltz-Rubenach'. We stood waiting like pilgrims outside this House Wonderful, and presently we heard the unfastening of bolts. In the humour that possessed us, we should not have been surprised if the opening of the door had revealed a porter in the form of a three-headed dragon. I fancy we should have bowed before him. But the spell was partly broken when a mild-faced woman appeared and asked for the Count's permission to view the Schloss. Having received it, she took us to another door opening on to the courtyard, and gravely handed us over to the show-woman of the enchanted palace, a very buxom dame who proved to be as good-natured as she was fat. She bade us leave our umbrellas on a seat outside the door, and then led us 'upstairs, downstairs, in my lady's chamber', through a most bewildering series of quaint rooms, full of objects of interest, with rare furniture of two and three centuries and more ago. …

We went up and down, turned and twisted, from chamber to chamber along dark and narrow passages, now to right, then to left. Once a steep flight of stairs, with angles near doorways big enough to hold two persons suggesting treason and eavesdropping, led down into a good-sized bedroom.

We were shown the bedroom and the dressing rooms of the young Count and Countess, who spend a fortnight every year at the castle. The bed hangings were very interesting, the door had huge solid-looking silver hinges. These our guide told us were modern; most of the furniture was very old. The Countess's toilet-chamber, too, was quaintly old-fashioned; but the views from the windows were lovely and varied, commanding constantly changing views of the winding and beautiful Elz valley. We saw the children's rooms and the guest chambers: one of these had its four-post bedstead in carved oak, with beautiful silk hangings. Out of one large room a chapel or oratory opened with an altar, and painted glass windows. The bed in the room itself looked gruesome, and had a flight of steps on one side to enable its occupants to reach the deep box which held the bedding. There was something uncanny about it and its quaint, sombre hangings; one felt that a mystery might have happened in this chamber, and that it might be haunted. We saw another room with several beds, bright and cherry-looking, and we were told that it was the hospital-chamber.

Then we visited the Fahnensaal with its rich vaulted roof and its charming oriel, or Ecke; the dining-room contained several family portraits; the Kurfürstensaal, the Rustkammer, the boudoir of the lady of the house, with some family-portraits; above all, the Rittersaal. … The greater number of the bedrooms are of moderate size; many of them have bare, unpolished oak flooring with here and there a strip of carpet. The prevailing tone of the house is that of a rigorous, and in some cases, almost grim simplicity, wonderfully suggestive of the later Middle Ages."

View into the inner courtyard

The 20th Century

What began in the 19th century continued in the 20th century. The German Emperor William II visited Eltz Castle in 1906. The number of visitors increased to such an extent, that the rather complicated regulation of applying in writing for a permit to visit the castle had to be given up. Instead, regular opening hours were introduced. The Baedeker of 1925, for example, writes about Eltz Castle: "the courtyard is open to the public; the interior can only be visited during the owner's absence on weekdays 9–12 and 2–6." The entrance fee was one Mark.

The first small castle guide was published as early as 1931 by Johanna Countess Erwein zu Eltz. It contains a brief description of the different buildings and a history of the family. The author justified the publication of the brochure with the "general interest shown by frequent visitors to Eltz Castle and its surrounding." Her concern is also to "rectify the often incorrect stories about the fire of 1920", and she promises a description of the tragic events of 1920 "according to the oral report of the castle administrator Miss Lieschen Hendgen and 'Oberrentmeister' Schreckenberg." According to this description, a fire broke out in the night of 26 September 1920 in the Kempenich Houses, which could at first not be brought under control. Even though "helpers and the hand pump were available immediately [and] the caretaker Hartung and the forester Wisniewski were at the site straight away," the fire spread quickly. "Finally the fire brigade arrived, but was unable to bring their large pumps because of the steep hill. They had to use the hand pump and a long chain of people passing buckets of water up from the Eltz river. Helpers and onlookers had hurried to the site from the nearby villages." By the time the fire was finally put out with the help of the people from the nearby villages, most of the Kempenich Houses as well as parts of the Platt-Eltz and the upper floors of the Rodendorf Houses had been destroyed. Only Rübenach House remained unscathed. The restora-

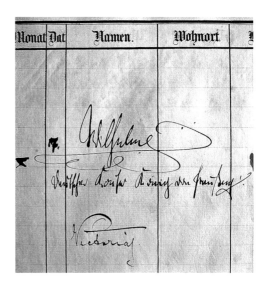

The entry of Emperor William II in the guestbook of Eltz Castle

tion works began in the same year and progressed well at first. Work came to a standstill in 1923, however because of "lack of money and inflation" – as Johanna Countess Erwein zu Eltz puts it. It was not before 1927 that the castle administrator, who lived provisionally in the little goldsmith's house – today the upper restaurant – was able to move back into her apartment in one of the Kempenich Houses. The restoration was completed in 1930. As most of the furniture had been rescued from the flames, many of the rooms were restored to the way they were before the fire.

During the Second World War the sheltering walls of the castle played a role that was almost reminiscent of medieval times. Several families, who had been evacuated from endangered villages, were temporarily housed in the remote castle.

Romantic traditions were revived in the second half of the 20th century and Eltz Castle became an increasingly popular tourist attraction. A souvenir shop and two restaurants opened on the grounds of the outer bailey. The upper restaurant is in a former craftsman's cottage, the lower one in the former carriage house. Extensive repair works were under-

WER BANKNOTEN NACHMACHT
ODER VERFÄLSCHT
ODER NACHGEMACHTE ODER VERFÄLSCHTE
SICH VERSCHAFFT
UND IN VERKEHR BRINGT,
WIRD MIT FREIHEITSSTRAFE
NICHT UNTER ZWEI JAHREN
BESTRAFT

V 8047998 T

The reverse of the 500-Mark banknote, used from April 1965 to June 1995

taken in the 1970s and early 1980s, which included works to secure the bastions to the west of the castle. At this time the cellars of Rübenach House were also renovated and converted into a museum, the so-called treasure vault. The exhibits include weapons, jewellery, beautifully crafted gold, porcelain and a vast variety of artworks owned by the Eltz family. The treasure vault was opened in 1981. Until the 1990s, a banknote was the most prominent advertisement for Eltz Castle – it adorned the verso of the old 500 Mark note. Today the castle is one of the most popular tourist attractions in Germany. More than 300 000 visitors from Germany and abroad visit the castle each year. Today, like 850 years ago, Eltz Castle is still owned by the family of the same name. The present owner, Dr. Count Karl von und zu Eltz-Kempenich, genannt Faust von Stromberg, represents the 33rd generation. He lives in Eltville on the Rhine, where the Eltz family has owned a residence since the 17th century. Caretakers have lived in Eltz Castle permanently for more than two hundred years.

A Journey through the Centuries:
The Interior

While the Platt-Eltz and the Kempenich Houses are today privately used, large parts of Rübenach House and the Rodendorf Houses are open to the public. Guided tours take visitors through the rooms, allowing insights into the life in Eltz Castle and leaving an unforgettable impression of late medieval living culture in the Rhineland. All the furniture and artworks in the castle belong to the Eltz family.

The Entrance Hall

The tour through the castle starts in the entrance hall of Rübenach House. This rather sombre room was once the reception hall. It was only converted into an armoury in recent years (fig. right). It would have been unthinkable in medieval times to keep weapons in any of the residential parts of the castle. They were usually locked away in separate rooms. The Rübenach entrance hall was probably refurbished in the 19th century to suit the fashion of the time.

The left side of the room is dominated by a closed spiral staircase leading to the upper floors of Rübenach House. At the rear, between the staircase and the windows, is a simple Gothic fireplace crowned by the Eltz coat of arms with the Silver Lion. A complete suit of armour hangs on the west wall above the windows alongside several cuirasses, burgonets and attack helmets. Unlike the burgonet, the latter had no visor and was worn when attacking a castle. It protected the wearer against stones, missiles or hot pitch that was poured down from the castle. Other pieces of a foot soldier's armour displayed here are a round shield and a chain mail, an additional protec-

tion worn under the cuirass. A closer look shows that it consists of small metal rings that are bound together with string.

A couple of simple missiles like heavy arrows hang to the left of the windows. They date from the 14th century, the time of the Eltz Feud. The upper bolts were fired from large crossbows, the lower ones from an earlier type of firearm which looked like the reconstruction hanging below the arrows. The Trier Elector Balduin of Luxemburg must have used such early weapons during the siege of Eltz Castle.

Among the firearms is a so-called arkebuse to the right of the window. These 15th-century

The entrance hall with weapons and the Eltz-Rübenach coat of arms above the fireplace

Halberds in the entrance hall of Rübenach House

firearms had a large hook below the barrel, which was rammed into ramparts or walls in order stop the recoil. Arkebuses were cast out of bronze or forged out of iron. They were mostly used for defence purposes.

More advanced examples of these early firearms can be seen along the timber-frame wall on the right. They are matchlocks and wheellocks, which were muzzle-loaded with gunpowder and shot and are therefore also called muzzleloaders. The powder in the older matchlocks was ignited with a piece of woollen string soaked in saltpetre known as a "match". As the saltpetre gave off a characteristic smell when lit, it often alerted the enemy. The German expression "Lunte riechen" (literally "smell the match"), meaning to become suspicious, refers to this. It is only one of 800 German proverbs and expressions that have their origins in the world of medieval castles. Soon after its invention in the 15th century the

matchlock began to be improved. Its successor was the so-called wheellock, which was first produced in Nuremberg around 1515. Two examples of this weapon can be seen in the entrance hall below the matchlocks. The wheellocks have a simple mechanism, in which a wheel spins against a flint creating sparks that ignite the powder. A wheellock was more complicated to make and therefore four times as expensive as a matchlock. It was much more reliable, however. The wheellock was built and sold for more than two hundred years; it was even used in some hunting rifles up to the 18th century.

To the right of the matchlocks and wheellocks is a collection of oriental weapons including daggers, a ceremonial or parade sword made out of the jaw of a swordfish, a light round shield made of silk, riding boots, quivers as well as several bows and arrows. They were all seized by members of the Eltz family during the Turkish Wars in the 17th and 18th century, probably during the Turkish siege of Vienna in 1683.

Finally, below the matchlocks and wheellocks and the oriental weapons, is a row of halberds. They were the typical pole weapons of ordinary foot soldiers and consisted of a wooden shaft with an axe blade topped with a long spike, the so-called "pike", and a hook, which was used to draw horsemen to the ground. The armed foot soldiers, also known as "Pikiere" (or: pikers) were the lowest ranking members of a military force. Whoever began his military career as a foot soldier would later say he had learned his profession "von der Pike aufwärts" (from the pike upwards), as a German expression goes.

The Rübenach Lower Hall

A low door leads from the entrance hall into the Rübenach lower hall, a large, comfortable living room (fig. p. 42) that is nearly unchanged. The plain oak ceiling still dates from the 15th century, the time the house was built. Only the mighty beam supporting the ceiling was added during restoration works in the 19th century. Before then the ceiling here and on the upper floors was supported by a central pillar.

The lower hall in Rübenach House was heated by an open fireplace – as were forty of the one hundred rooms in the castle. This unusually large number of fireplaces shows how comfortable the buildings in Eltz Castle were. Like in the entrance hall, the fireplace is crowned by the coat of arms of the family Eltz of the Silver Lion. Standing in the hearth are so-called fire dogs which supported the logs to prevent them from rolling into the room. The cast iron fireback on the rear wall of the fireplace stored and radiated the heat long after the fire had gone out. Such iron plates were often inserted in a wall between two rooms in order to heat both rooms with only one fire.

The fireback in the Rübenach lower hall was made in 1537 in the Eifel. The floor of the hearth is made of vertical slabs of slate over a layer of sand. They, too, stored heat like the fireback. This type of hearth had the further advantage over stone slabs that it could not crack in the heat. Another central element of this hall are the windows in addition to the fireplace. As lighting in medieval rooms was sparse – in this sense the Middle Ages were truly a dark age – people made the best use of daylight. Benches were built into the wide alcoves in order to use the daylight until sunset. At night the castle and the windowless passage ways were lit mostly with pinewood torches, which were held by table supports or iron rings on the walls. Talcum lamps or torches were also popular, while candles were not very common as they were extremely expensive and burned down quickly. Candles were used in the original antler chandelier above the table, which is made out of antlers and has a female figure with a fish tail like a Mermaid's holding a coat

16th-century folding chair

Chandelier made of antlers in the Rübenach lower hall

of arms. Chandeliers like this one were popular in Germany in the 15th century; the Baroque shape of the coat of arms is an indication that the chandelier was altered at a later date.

The windows are glazed with crown glass – a typical feature in wealthy houses in the 15th century. This simple form of window glass was made by blowing a glass bulb which was then pressed – or spun – while still hot until it was flat and round. The breaking point of the glass blower's pipe can still be seen in the centre of the panes. The uncut panes were secured in lead. This type of glazing was known already in the ancient Roman Empire, but only came to central Europe during the Crusades. In early medieval architecture windows were usually closed with wooden shutters, cloth soaked in talcum, parchment or sometimes also animal skins.

The furniture in the Rübenach lower hall dates from different centuries. Originally, the room was more sparsely furnished than today. Furniture was precious in the Middle Ages and only the most necessary items were bought. The most important piece of furniture was the chest, which was used to store clothing or utensils as well as to sit on. It was also used for transportation, as a table, or – covered with pillows – even as a bed. At first chests were made out of hollowed tree trunks, which were increasingly replaced by box chests ("Betttruhen"). In the course of time these chests were also decorated. The metal fittings, which were originally mere reinforcements, became more and more elaborate, and the front of the chest was often adorned with woodcarvings or paintings. The large chest in the Rübenach lower hall standing against the windowless east wall facing the inner courtyard dates from this period. The late Gothic chest is decorated with plant ornaments. 15 pewter jugs of different sizes dating from the 17th to the 18th century are arranged on top of the chest.

The late Gothic clock from southern Germany a couple of metres to the right of the chest dates from the 15th century. Its painted face bears the date 1483 as well as the Eltz coat of arms. This means that the clock was presumably made for a member of the Eltz family. The clock was probably converted into a pendulum clock in the 17th century.

The 16th-century folding chair standing in the same corner is one of the oldest chairs in the castle (fig. p. 45). The folding chair, like the chest, was a mobile piece of furniture that could easily be transported. The history of this practical piece of furniture goes back to antiquity. It was common among the Egyptians as well as the ancient Greeks and Romans. It was most popular in medieval castles and towns

before being replaced by upholstered armchairs in Baroque times.

The two predominantly green Flemish tapestries on the east wall date from around 1580 (fig. p. 48/49). While tapestries were originally used only for insulation and for creating a warmer atmosphere in medieval rooms, they increasingly also served more decorative purposes. The two tapestries here show animals and plants, some of which seem rather exotic. This reflects a fashion at a time when Europeans began exploring other continents and images of strange cultures and artworks began to spread.

Late Gothic chest with 17th and 18th-century pewter jugs

Some of the castle's most beautiful and best preserved paintings can also be seen here. To the left on the timber-frame wall to the entrance hall hangs a panel depicting The Mass of St. Gregory by the Cologne school of painters. It is dated 1494 and was presumably the right panel of an altarpiece. This was no unusual motif in the 15th century. It shows Pope Gregory the Great celebrating the Mass in a Gothic church interior when Christ appears, bleeding from all his wounds and squirting blood into a chalice. The scene was intended to demonstrate the miracle of conversion – the transformation of holy wine into blood. Other motifs from the Passion of Christ appear in the background, such as the Kiss of Judas, Torturers and their Implements, St. Peter and the Cock, The Ladder for the Deposition, the Torn Curtain of the Temple in Jerusalem and, at the front on the right, the instruments Pilate used to wash his hands. To medieval viewers this was a story about the transformation and its backgrounds. Even though perspective had been discovered by painters in Italy by this time, the painter of this panel was obviously not yet familiar with these achievements. His perspective is purely emotional, as we can see in the outlines of the altar, which move outwards.

To the right of this, above the door to the entrance hall, is a much smaller panel painting showing the Adoration of the Magi. It, too, was painted by the Cologne school of painters around 1500.

Slightly further to the right is a Madonna painted around 1520 by Lucas Cranach the Elder (fig. p. 51). A tiny snake, the artist's emblem, is recognisable on the right of the painting. It shows the Virgin Mary handing the Infant Jesus some grapes. Her blond hair is hidden beneath a transparent veil covering her forehead down to her eyes. It is a symbol of innocence. Her dress is dark red, the colour of the heavenly queen, but also of the blood her son Jesus will shed. Mary's cloak is blue and green – blue as the symbol of loyalty and the colour of heaven where she will be accepted, green as the sign of hope and the colour of spring, rebirth and Paradise. The grapes are a reference to the Bible: *"I am the vine; you are the branches. Anyone who dwells in me, as I dwell in him, bears much fruit …"* The motif of Mary with her child and grapes was popular in devotional and meditation pictures in the 15th and 16th century. No background distracts from Mary and Jesus, nothing to distract from our devotion.

The Crucifixion between the windows was painted in 1495 also by the same Cologne school of painters. The setting of the Crucifixion has been transferred from Palestine to central Europe. The hilly landscape dotted with castles should have been a familiar sight

The Mass of St. Gregory, Cologne school of painters, 1494

Madonna by Lucas Cranach the Elder, around 1520

Book illustration, probably from the workshop of Michael Pacher, around 1550

to people in late-medieval Germany. Beneath the cross on the right is a group of four women with St. John, on the left are some soldiers. A knight stands next to the Cross, looking up at Christ. There is a small crown and the inscription "Elz" on his thigh, an indication that this painting was commissioned by a member of the Eltz family.

At the other end of the room, to the left of the fireplace, is an Adoration scene by the school of Lucas Cranach. On the right is a book illustration made presumable by the workshop of the South Tyrol painter Michael Pacher in the early 16th century.

The Rübenach Bed Chamber

A narrow spiral staircase leads from the Rübenach lower hall to a large bedroom on the upper floor. The modern name of this room is not entirely correct, as in the Middle Ages rooms were usually used for both living and sleeping in. This large, representational room was, therefore, probably not only a bed chamber, but also a communal living room.

The most striking features in this room are the colourful murals on the walls and the wooden ceiling. It is rare for such decorations to have survived in a medieval castle, as most were lost as a result of later alterations. The overall pattern of blossoms, fruits, leaves and vines in this room has a slightly Oriental touch. Plant motifs like these were indeed imported from the Orient after European crusaders made their first encounters with Arabic art. The murals in the Rübenach bed chamber date from the construction period of Rübenach House in the 15th century and were restored in the late 19th century.

The late Gothic chapel oriel in the east wall of the room also dates from this period. The small chapel had to be built into an oriel as no one was supposed to live above a church. As there were several floors above the Rübenach bed chamber, the altar was placed outside of the room in an oriel jutting out into the inner courtyard. It has a delicate net vault and the stained glass windows and the murals to the left and right of the altar are particularly colourful. The brilliant stained glass windows – like a medieval slide – depict the Adoration of the Magi at the top, a motif that is repeated in parts on the woven altar curtain. The lower

The Rübenach bed chamber with 15th-century murals

The builder of Rübenach House Wilhelm von Eltz with his coat of arms

Wilhelm's wife Katharina von Eltz, nee Blankart von Ahrweiler

Mural in the Rübenach chapel oriel

windows show the coat of arms of the line Eltz of the Silver Lion surrounded by the kneeling donors: left Wilhelm von Eltz, the builder of Rübenach House in a suit of armour, right his wife Katharina von Eltz, nee Blankart von Ahrweiler. The murals in the oriel depict a Crucifixion scene on the left and a Descent from the Cross on the right. The chapel oriel could be closed off with two painted doors.

The centre of the spacious bedroom is taken up by a large wooden bed with a canopy. It is 2.20 metres long and 1.75 metres wide and was made around 1520. The bed is raised on several steps in order to benefit from the rising warmth in the room. There was a wide fireplace in the opposite wall, but it would never really have sufficed to heat this high room in winter. The canopy and the curtains were, therefore, an additional shelter against the cold. The bedding consisted of linen sheets, pillows and blankets filled with hair, wool or down. The wooden moulding at the top of the bed displays painted hunting and tournament

Chapel oriel with stained glass windows, 15th century

scenes; two family coats of arms adorn the fronts, one of them is the coat of arms of the Eltz family.

Another interesting piece of furniture is the dark-brown cabinet-on-stand ("Stollen-schrank") on the south wall between the doors leading to the adjoining rooms. It was made in Cologne around 1560. A cabinet-on-stand is a cross between a chest and a wardrobe: a chest placed on legs so that it could be opened without bending over. The front is beautifully carved with Biblical scenes of the story of Samson.

A wooden alcove in the north-west corner of the bed chamber hides a small latrine. The wooden interior dates from the 19th century, but the oriel itself goes back to the time the house was built. Medieval toilet pipes were sometimes made of wood, sometimes out of stone like here and led from the latrine down the wall of the building before ending in a pit. In order to clean these shafts, rainwater was directed from the roofs through the shafts, a simple predecessor of modern water closets. Instead of toilet paper, medieval people – according to a Zurich manuscript of the 15th century – used hay or cabbage leaves. Eltz castle possessed a total of twenty private latrines – like the large number of fireplaces another indication of the high level of comfort in this castle.

Latrine in the Rübenach bed chamber

The Dressing Room and the Study

Two smaller rooms adjoin the Rübenach bed chamber. The dressing room on the right is decorated in a similar fashion to the large bed chamber with well-preserved late-Gothic murals covering the walls and ceiling, even the window recess, the stair tower and the fireplace. The colours are similar to those in the bed chamber, with a predominance of green vines with colourful fruits and blossoms. Here there are also figural scenes entwined in the vines, however. To the right of the window, for example, is a knight and his wife with two female attendants all dressed in 15th-century fashions (fig. p. 58). An inscription above the male figure reads: "Anno Domini 1451" and above the woman "Jutta von Eltz Herren Lanzelots Hausfrau". To the left of the window is another similarly clothed couple with the inscriptions "Wilhelm Herr zu Eltz" and "Katharina Blankartin von Ahrweiler". And finally, on the south wall, a knight hands a ring to a lady in a courtly dress; between them stands a slender tree, probably a Tree of Life (fig. back cover).

The furniture in this room all dates from the 19th century. There is a neo-Gothic chest of drawers on the left and two tables, among

Dressing room with murals, 15th century

them on the right a simple washing table with washing utensils. Like the furniture, the name of the room as a dressing room probably goes back no further than the 19th century and is a reference to the depictions of medieval fashions.

The cosy study with wood panelling on the walls is entirely a creation of Romanticism. When Karl Count zu Eltz-Kempenich had Eltz Castle restored in the 19th century (cf. p. 30), he employed the painter Eduard Knackfuß, whose father had worked for the Eltz family and in Eltz Castle, to restore the murals in the bed chamber and the dressing room. While these two rooms only needed conservational measures, Count Karl had the small Study fac-

ing the inner courtyard completely refurbished for his wife Countess Ludwine. "For me its was merely the realisation of a particular idea of the Count's", wrote the painter in his memoirs about this commission: "In itself already a pretty, cosy room with a bay window and wooden panelling on the walls, he envisaged a room decorated in the style of the Archbishop Wolf Drietrich room in the old archbishopric palace in Salzburg with murals in a late-Gothic style. He even had small-scale copies made in watercolour for this purpose. The Salzburg murals showed fantastic, stylised green vines with large colourful flowers on a dark, almost black background. Small individual figures had been added. Following the ornamental forms,

People in 15th-century fashions in the murals in the dressing room

Murals in the study with figurative images showing the children of Count Karl zu Eltz

The Study with 19th-century murals

it was my task to fill the decorative wall segments with my own compositions. I wanted to give the figurative element a greater presence than in the original." Eduard Knackfuß, at that time a student at the Düsseldorf Art Academy, spent some time in Eltz Castle in the summer of 1881 to complete the task. It was done in a style that takes up the decorative vine ornaments in the bed chamber with the addition of

portraits of Count Karl and his children: "the count wanted everything to appear cheerful and friendly. My father therefore told me to strive for an effect like the foliage of a beech forest in the sunlight, the blue sky visible through the leaves. In the figurative parts I depicted the members of the count's family in a style to suit the ornamental character of the whole. The main wall showed the two sons of

The painter Eduard Knackfuß dedicated his murals in the study to the landlady, 1881

the count as hunters, following their game with hunting spears and crossbows and clothed like the other figures in 15th-century fashions. The countesses found their place on the side walls, some full-length, one with a falcon, another with a lute, the others half-length, rising up out of calyces", writes Knackfuß.

The Electors Room

A staircase leads from the Rübenach bed chamber into the neighbouring Groß-Rodendorf House, which one enters through the well-lit Electors room. The unusual, hexagonal shape of this room shows to what extent the castle architecture had to adapt to the natural rock formation. The buildings follow the shape of the rocks on which they stand. The Electors room is the only room open to the public that was destroyed in the fire in 1920 (cf. p. 40). Before the fire, an armchair of Elector Jakob III von Eltz of Trier stood in this room, giving it its name. Today two portraits commemorate the two electors in the Eltz family. The one depicts the mentioned Jakob III, while the other shows Philipp Karl von Eltz, who was Elector and Archbishop of Mainz in the mid 18th century, and thus also "Erbkanzler" (Archicancellarius) of the Holy Roman Empire of German Nations (cf. pp. 26–28), the second most important man in the country after the Emperor.

After passing through the medieval-style rooms in Rübenach House, the Electors room takes visitors into a later period. The furniture consists of a Baroque wardrobe from southern Germany with elaborately turned columns, a 16th-century Renaissance chest and four Rococo chairs. The chairs with their elaborate, asymmetrical ornaments are probably Flemish and date from the 18th century. The optical centre of the room is the large tapestry on the rear wall in shades of green. It was made around 1680 in the workshop of the brothers von der Brüggen in Brussels. The tapestry depicts Autumn, represented by a hunting scene with dogs and a hunter about to leave on a hunt. Weapons such as hunting spears and pointed staffs for hunting boar lean against columns. Above is a garland with autumn fruits and a ram's head, a symbol of fertility.

To the right of the fireplace is an engraving showing the signing of the Peace of Westphalia, which was attended by a lord of Eltz as the representative of the elector of Trier (fig. p. 27). A collection of coloured 18th and 19th-century

The Electors room with a tapestry of 1680

Chinese porcelain is presented further to the right in a small niche. The niche is flanked by two small shrines made in the workshop of the Bavarian sculptor family Schwanthaler. They depict the Agony in the Garden and the Deposition.

The Knights Hall

The knights hall is the largest room in the castle, covering one entire floor of the Groß-Rodendorfer House. It has two fireplaces. The dark red tapestries, imprinted with the family coat of arms, are of a more recent date. Still, they bring to mind that it was common practice to cover the cold walls of such large rooms that could hardly be heated comfortably in order to store the warmth.

The hall with four large windows on its eastside served as a festival and assembly hall for the members of the "Ganerben"-community on Burg Eltz. Several symbols that are easily overlooked give an insight into the practices at

Rococo chairs in the Electors room

tury, the assembly hall, too, was altered during the restoration works in this period. The three 16th-century suits of armour along the window front were put on display here in the 19th century. The so-called Maximilian's suit of armour in the centre is the best preserved. The name of this type of armour goes back to Emperior Maximilian I, who is referred to as the "last German knight". This one is reported to have belonged to Johann Anton zu Eltz from the line of the Golden Lion. It was made around 1520. The striking corrugations improved the stability of the armour, thus optimising the safety of the person inside. The disadvantage of such suits of armour was their enormous weight: They weighed around 60 pounds. When wearing his suit of armour the knight was unable to mount his horse without help – he needed several helpers or even a windlass to lift him onto his horse.

At the far end of the knights hall, in front of the right fireplace, are a number of model cannons, fully functioning, small-scale copies of

the assemblies that were held here. Small faces faintly reminiscent of court jesters, so-called jester's masks, can be seen beneath the heavy ceiling beam and in some corners of the room. They are an indication that this room allowed freedom of speech, meaning that everyone could express their opinions openly. The pointed arch on the doorway, on the other hand, is crowned by the red rose of silence, an appeal not to talk about the discussed issues after leaving the hall.

The whole interior of this room creates a ceremonious, formal atmosphere. The coats of arms of the Eltz family and related noble families are presented in a frieze below the wooden ceiling. The furnishing of the hall with suits of armour, weapons and other military implements is an idea of Romanticism. Like the entrance hall in Rübenach House, which was transformed into an armoury in the 19th cen-

Model canons in the knights hall

The knights hall was a festival and assembly hall

real cannons. Such copies were made by gun founders to show their customers the different types of cannons they could make en miniature. They were later often fired in salute at various occasions. Next to these are three iron boxes reminiscent of strong boxes dating from the late 16th century. A single key inserted in the lock in the middle of the heavy lid moved seven bolts at once. On the opposite wall hangs a large portrait of Emperor Leopold I, a reminder that the mother of the present owner of Eltz Castle is a descendent of the House of Habsburg.

Finally, there is the colourful tapestry made around 1700 in the royal manufacture Gobelin in Paris. It depicts a scene from Greek mythology, namely the Greek sun god Helios dining with his wife and sister, the moon goddess Selene, surrounded by the nine Muses. At the time when the French king called himself Sun King, this scene from Antiquity was topical. This is evident also in the fact that the food,

the implements and the pieces of architecture are typical of the 17th century rather than Antiquity. The scene shown on the tapestry could be set at a royal court in Baroque times.

A spiral stairway leads to the floor below the knights hall. Spiral staircases, which in Eltz Castle were mostly made from grey basalt or – like in the knights hall – red sandstone, were

Jester's mask in the knights hall

Detail of the tapestry in the knights hall, made around 1700 by the Royal manufacture Gobelin in Paris

The tapestry depicts the Greek sun god Helios at a feast

typical features of castles for several reasons. Spiral staircases are extremely stable and they take up little space. More important, however, was that they facilitated the defence of the castle. At least before 1700 such stairs always descended in a counter-clockwise direction, giving the defender free swing of his sword in his right hand, while the aggressor was obstructed by the central newel.

Spiral staircase in Groß-Rodendorf House

The Angel room is furnished in the style of a hunting room according to the Romanticist fashion at the time

The Angel Room and Wamboldt Room

Descending from the knights hall, the visitor first enters a narrow, dark timber-frame passage, which leads on into the so-called Angel room. The wooden floor in a geometric design was reconstructed in 1984 after original fragments found here. Unlike the more festive knights hall, this room really looks lived-in. The wooden floor and the scattered bear skins create a very homely atmosphere. The room is furnished as a hunting room in the style of Romanticism. We can see a number of trophies, including the mighty antlers of a moose shot by a member of the Eltz family in the early 20th century in Alaska, as well as a collection of

hunting weapons of the 18th and 19th century. The furniture includes an 18th-century table, perhaps originally a gaming table. It is decorated with beautiful inlay depicting motifs from rural life and hunting to suit the room. Here, too, a tapestry is hung above the fireplace. These decorative, woven curtains adorned fireplaces during the summer months when they were not in use.

The following Wamboldt room is a bright and friendly room named after the Wamboldt family in Umstadt. There were several marriages between members of the Eltz family and the Wamboldt family in the course of the centuries. Today the room is furnished like a housewife's workroom in the 18th century, with a laundry press, a spinning wheel and a reel for thread or wool. Four plain 17th-century chairs from southern Germany stand around a table with a top of beautifully decorated limestone. A delicate pattern and the date 1703 are incised in the table top. An inlayed cupboard from Ulm and a Baroque cabinet-on-stand complete the furniture in this room. Small portraits of family members hang on the walls.

The Countesses Room

Right next door is the Countesses room. Despite the thick walls and the relatively small windows, this whitewashed room is very bright (fig. p. 68). Walls and ceilings plastered with clay and whitewashed were already common in the early days of the castle. Not only were the rooms brighter, but this technique also prevented fires from spreading quickly. Even the floor of the Countesses room is covered with a

In the Wamboldt room

clay-like plaster of limestone, which was painted red.

The name Countesses room – or nursery – is probably newer and refers to the pictures of children adorning the room. They date from the 18th century and depict the children of the Eltz family. As was the fashion in that period, the children are shown dressed like little adults in stiff, artificial poses. The little girl to the right above the door to the Wamboldt room, for example, is portrayed as a shepherdess. Two other features promote the assumption that this room was once a nursery. Firstly a second, higher bench was installed in the right window niche, which is far too narrow for an adult to sit on. Secondly, there is a narrow red ladder in the rear right corner of the room leading into another bedroom – perhaps that of the parents or a nurse. The most striking piece of furniture is the painted bridal bed, made around 1525 in the Würzburg region. It is considered the oldest Renaissance bed in Germany and is unusually large with a length of 2.05 metres and a width of 1.45 metres. There is also an 18th-cen-

Portrait of a child in the Countesses room

Collection of ceramics in the Countesses room

tury cot, a southern German chest of the same period and two screens made out of a 16th-century tapestry in shades of green. A ceramic collection is presented in a large niche in the wall to the inner courtyard. The jugs are up to 400 years old and were produced in different central European ceramic manufacturing centres, including Siegburg, Frechen, Raeren, Creusen, Delft and the Westerwald.

A cuirass, a glove and a battle axe in the left corner above the entrance to the latrine seem out of place in this context. Legend has it that the cuirass belonged to a daughter of the Eltz family, the hero of the only known saga about Eltz Castle. The historian Friedrich Wilhelm Roth repeats this saga in his book about the "History of the Lords and Counts of Eltz as follows":

"At an unknown time a gentleman of Braunsberg became engaged to Agnes, daughter of Eltz, and the event was celebrated in the knights hall of Eltz Castle with a feast and wine. Agnes refused to kiss the drunken groom, who was insulted and challenged the family. The watchfulness of the Eltz inhabitants rendered all his attempts to damage the Eltz family futile. One day, however, when Agnes' father rode out to hunt, the Braunsberg gentleman attacked the castle with his men, but failed to gain entrance because Agnes had taken charge of the remaining servants and defended the castle. Furious, he shot his former fiancée with

Countesses room with a painted bridal bed, around 1525

his gun. It is said that he never found his peace after his death and that he wanders around Agnes' grave at night."

The glove in the Countesses room is said to be the gauntlet thrown by the Braunsberg knight when he challenged Agnes' father and the cuirass part of the suit of armour Agnes wore when she died defending the castle.

The Banner Hall

Another spiral staircase leads from the Countesses room down into the banner hall on the ground floor. The name of this atmospheric room with its elaborate late Gothic vaulting probably originated in the late 19th century. Banners looted in the German-French War of 1870/71 were presumably displayed here for a few years after the 19th-century restoration. The elaborate vault and the small oriel in the east could lead to the assumption that this was once a chapel, or at least intended as such. This assumption is further supported by the fact that the two figures bearing coats of arms to the left and right of the oriel are actually angels. On the other hand, the room is furnished like a living room and elaborate vaults were not uncommon in the houses of wealthy citizens. The painter Eduard Knackfuß, who was in Eltz Castle several times during the restoration measures in the 1880s, wrote in his memoirs that the banner hall was used as a dining room when the owner, Karl Count of Eltz, was in the castle.

The late Gothic net vault gives this room a very elegant appearance. The stone ribs are not only decorative, but also have a supporting function. They were the first elements of the vault to be placed over a wooden construction. They were secured by the keystone before the scaffolding was removed and the sections between the ribs were filled. The cells in the banner hall are decorated with simple floral and vine patterns. The two keystones in the centre

Tiled stove in the banner hall, around 1881

of the vault bear the coats of arms of the Eltz family and other families related through marriage. We notice one coat of arms, in particular, which occurs on the vault, above the fireplace and in the oriel. The jagged red line belongs to the coat of arms of the Pyrmont family, which reminds us of Elisabeth of Pyrmont, the wife of Philipp von Eltz, the builder of Groß-Rodendorf House.

Not only the vault, but also the floor in this hall date from the early days of the castle. Some of the plain, reddish clay tiles with simple Gothic ornaments still recognisable in some places date back to the 13th century and were reused here.

There is a wood-panelled bay window in the east wall of the banner hall with a table and benches forming a comfortable seating area. These wooden pieces of furniture were built in the 1880s, while the windows are original. The stained glass window depicts St. George fighting the Dragon – a popular motif in castles, as

Stained glass window showing St. George

St. George was the patron saint of Christian knights. The console clock next to the oriel dates from the 16th century.

The tiled stove in the north wall is the most magnificent feature in the banner hall (fig. p. 69). It was commissioned in 1881 by Count Karl of Eltz after an almost identical stove of 1540 in the Germanisches Nationalmuseum in Nuremberg. Like on the stove in Nuremberg, the tiles here also depict Evangelists, but there are also members of the Eltz family and other relatives. The tiled stove was heated from the neighbouring kitchen in Groß-Rodendorf House.

Net vault in the banner hall

The banner hall with the wood-panelled oriel and a 16th-century console clock

Cooking in the late Middle Ages – the Rodendorf kitchen

The Rodendorf Kitchen

The kitchen, the last room of the tour, is only one of at least three kitchens in Eltz Castle. The houses of the different lines of the family each had their own kitchens supplying a total number of approximately 100 people. Like in other castles, only few medieval kitchen implements have survived due to their extensive use. Only the large, plain wooden chest to the right of the entrance, which was used to store flour, dates from the 15th century. The other pieces of furniture and utensils in the kitchen today are from the 18th and 19th century. They were selected to

recreate the character of a late medieval kitchen, however.

The room is entirely functional. The plain, grey stone floor was easy to clean. Iron rings on the vaulted ceiling were used to hang valuable food such as smoked or cured meat out of reach of rats and mice. Other supplies were stored in vats, simple vessels and pantries – an example of which can be seen in the left wall of the kitchen. Salt was kept in small niches near the fireplace, where it stayed dry. A practical and cool storage place for fresh food was the wall cupboard in the opposite corner of the kitchen. The niche with a wooden door was

carved out of the 2-metre-thick walls and used for vegetables and other fresh food.

Food was cooked over the enormous fireplace. The fire was large enough to cook, fry and roast at the same time. The copper pot in the fireplace is hung by a large pot-hook. These jagged hooks made it possible to hang pots higher or lower above the fire and thus to regulate the temperature. Other pots were placed directly into the fire on iron stands. There was no separate baking room, only a large oven next to the fireplace. It is made of tuff, a volcanic rock that stores heat extremely well. A fire of wood and brushwood was lit inside the

oven; the ashes were then removed to bake the bread in the hot oven.

The staple diet in medieval times consisted not only of bread but also of root vegetables and cabbage. Wealthy households like Eltz Castle would also have had plenty of meat and fish. Hunting, an exclusively aristocratic right, and the Eltz river provided the castle with meat and fish. There were also stables to the south of the castle where cattle was kept. Meat was chopped on a heavy chopping block that can still be seen in the kitchen on the right wall. Behind it is a sink with a drain leading out through the window recess. Water had to be carried here from the castle's only well in Kempenich House.

In the rear part of the kitchen to the right of the hearth is a servants' corner with neo-Gothic chairs and a table for the kitchen staff. The bronze and stone mortars were used to grind precious spices and the equally precious sugar.

The Chapel

After leaving Groß-Rodendorf House through the kitchen at the end of the tour, we come out right next to the entrance to the castle chapel, which is slightly concealed between the house and the passageway leading down to the gate. A narrow stair in the right wall of this passageway leads up into the chapel. The date of the first chapel in Eltz Castle is unknown, but

documents mention that the castle had a chapel as early as the early 14th century, which was furnished with a new altar in 1327. Friedrich Wilhelm Roth mentions this in his "History of the Lords and Counts of Eltz": "Bishop Arnold von Kamin, the son of Wilhelm of Eltz, was in Eltz on 20th August 1327 to consecrate the altar in the castle chapel, by special permission of Archbishop Baldewin of Trier, in honour of the Holy Trinity, the Holy Cross, the Virgin Mary and the Saints, particularly St. Pancras and St. Catherine, St. Andrew and St. Jacob the Elder, whose relics are enclosed in the altar. On behalf of Archbishop Baldewin he also dispensed indulgence for forty days to all those who confessed on each day of the month following the consecration and henceforth on the last day of each month for the first year and after that on each anniversary of the consecration."

St. Anna with Mary and Christ on her lap in the aisle of the chapel

Crucifixion group on the altar in the chapel

While most of the chapel interior dates from later centuries, a Gothic consecration cross out of tuff inserted in the central pillar on the left side of the nave indicates that this must be the original chapel mentioned in the passage quoted by Roth. The chapel has, however, been altered and restored several times since 1327. The date 1664 in the altar recess, for example, commemorates one of these alterations.

After mounting through the dark and narrow stairway, the chapel appears surprisingly bright and friendly with several windows and a white ceiling. The irregularly shaped aisle to the left of the nave is explained by the shape of the rock on which the castle is built. Oak benches for approximately thirty people stand on a plain basalt floor. The altar is in a small oriel with Gothic tracery windows.

The most beautiful artwork in the chapel is in the aisle. A late Gothic winged altar contains a painted wooden figure of St. Anne, the Virgin Mary and the Christ Child, the latter both sitting on St. Anne's lap. The wooden doors are painted, showing St. Margaret on the left and St. Gertrud as a Benedictine nun on the right. The precious monstrances and other liturgical implements that were used in the chapel are today kept in the treasure vault together with other precious items owned by the Eltz family.

The balcony on the rear wall of the chapel can be accessed from Rodendorf House. A small stair in the rear corner also links the chapel with the chaplain's room, which is today used as the sacristy. Throughout its history Eltz Castle nearly always had a resident chaplain, who lived in this room. This is no longer so today, but Mass is still celebrated during festivities and family gatherings. The present owner Karl Count von und zu Eltz-Kampenich, for example, married his Wife Countess Sophie von Schaffgotsch in the chapel of Eltz Castle.

A Cellar full of Precious Objects: The Treasure Vault

During the tour through the interior of the castle we are shown the residential rooms, an abundance of furniture, tapestries, paintings and a few weapons, but we see no small objects and trinkets, such as jewellery, table clocks, glasses, cutlery, coins or candle holders. While all these treasures could never be shown in the past for reasons of security, they are today exhibited on the lower floors of Rübenach House. Five rooms on four floors in the cellar of this house were converted into a museum during the renovation works in the 1970s and 1980s. The museum was inaugurated in 1981 by the German President Karl Carstens and houses more than 500 exhibits from the 12th to the 19th century, all of which were owned and once used by members of the Eltz family.

The Large Hall

The first room of the treasure vault is accessed by a short stair. It is a light, spacious hall with a floor of grey basalt and a plastered wooden ceiling supported by two stone columns. This room lies directly beneath the Rübenach lower hall, one of the main living rooms we saw during the tour of the interior, and offers a beautiful view over the western Eltz valley.

The most striking exhibit in this room is a statue of 1.1 metres in height depicting St. John of Nepomuk. The Baroque statue is made of silver and partly gilded. It was made in 1752 by the famous silversmith Franz Christoph Mäderl in Augsburg and stands on a richly decorated black base with the donor's coat of arms. John Nepomuk is occasionally referred to as the silent martyr as he refused to break

Silver statue of St. John of Nepomuk, 1752

Missal of the Mainz Elector Philipp Karl zu Eltz with his coat of arms the seal of confession and is known as a "bridge saint". He has been the patron saint of the Eltz family ever since the family's connection with the Faust von Stromberg family (cf. p. 29). Each male family member is traditionally named after him. An inscription on the reverse of the halo tells us how the statue came to the Eltz Family: *"Anno 1752 haben diese bildtnus des heyligen joannis von nepomuk vor die familie zur verehrung machen lassen anselm casimir frantz graff und edler Herr von Eltz Kempenich chur-mayntzischer und trierischer geheimbliche Ratth, Obrist Cammerer und Erbmarschall mit seiner Gemahlin Maria Joanna Freiyin Faust von Sromberg letztere des stames mit dem ausdrücklichen Vorbehalt das nimer mehr aus der familie von Eltz diese bildtnus abgegeben warden sole wieget ahn Silber 65 Marck/gekost/das Marck 15 Rthlr macht in geldtz 1565 gulden Rheinisch."* (rough translation: Anselm Casimir Frantz had this image of St. John Nepomuk made in 1752 for Count von Eltz-Kempenich, privy councillor of Mainz and Trier, treasurer and marshal and his wife Maria Joanna Baroness Faust von Stromberg under the condition that it shall never leave the Eltz family. The silver weighs 65 Marks, the equivalent to 1565 Rhenish Guilders).

The first display cases hanging on the right wall between the windows contain objects owned by the Elector and Archbishop of Mainz, Philipp Karl zu Eltz. The miniature in the first vitrine, for instance, was made in 1740 and shows a portrait of the Elector. There are further: a sextant made in 1735 in Dresden and a gold-plated gunpowder container made out of cast silver. The flat relief on the front depicts horses in battle, a representation of the victory of Christianity over the Ottomans. A medical instrument made of glass was used to bleed patients; the case for this instrument bears the electoral coat of arms of Philipp Carl. Most unusual are the two rings displayed in the centre of the vitrine. They were made for the Elector around 1730 in Idar-Oberstein. The two bezels out of gold-plated silver are plain frames for 49 colourful stones that could be exchanged to

Rings with interchangeable stones

suit the clothing or the mood of the day. A knife and fork with agate grips were also produced in Idar-Oberstein. The lower part of the display case contains Philipp Karl's travel accessories: a gold-plated bowl with a lid and saucer as well as a travelling cutlery set consisting of an ivory spoon, a knife and a fork with ivory grips. Left of this is a rapier, and on the right a walking stick that belonged to the Elector. The grip contains a watch that could be folded out. The lid of the grip is made out of gold-plated silver and bears the Elector's coat of arms worked in enamel.

The objects in the second vitrine also belonged to Philipp Karl and reflect the Elector's piety and interest in art. At the top are two late Baroque travel altars. These tiny altars of only a few centimetres height are made with great care and love of detail and are well worth a closer look. Beautiful gold artefacts are inlayed with diamonds, rubies and other precious stones. Painted miniatures on ivory appear through polished rock crystal. The paint-

Late Baroque travelling altar owned by Elector Philipp Karl

Glass collection, including glasses with coats of arms owned by Elector Philipp Karl

ing of the left – smaller – altar is flanked by silver columns, that of the right altar by four reddish agate columns (fig. p. 79). The same display case also contains a missal bound in red leather that was once owned by the Elector, a small Madonna made of gold-plated silver and a chalice, also of gold-plated silver and decorated with enamel, made in Salzburg around 1730.

The third display case also contains mostly clerical items. At the top is a Hungarian choral vestment decorated with red and gold appliqué work (around 1730). Below this is a tiny miniature of Hugo Franz zu Eltz, the Dean of the cathedral and a prayer book printed in Mainz in 1616 with an Eltz coat of arms embroidered on the velvet cover. At the bottom is a four-piece set of liturgical requisites (gold-plated silver) made in Augsburg in 1744 as well as a cross-shaped, gilded silver reliquary, beautifully decorated with precious stones.

A clock collection with a number of extremely original pieces is displayed in the fourth vitrine. At the top is a small cruciform clock with a casing made out of rock crystal set in gold-plated silver. It was made around 1585 in Augsburg and was a gift of Pope Sixtus V to the Trier Elector Jakob III zu Eltz. Below on the left is a figure clock from the period of the Thirty Years War. According to the mood at the time it shows an allegory of Peace with lowered weapons, bound warriors and a pair of heads above that are supposed to stand for reconciled enemies. Below this on the right is another table clock with a plain face at the top. It was made around 1700 in Frankfurt out of cast brass and then silver-plated and partly gilded. The table clock to the left of this is about one hundred years older and is made out of gold-plated copper. Four columns adorn the corners, supporting an oriental-style cupola. Finally, the most unusual clock in the collection,

Hoechst porcelain, 18th century

made in 1670 in Augsburg, is on the lowest tier. It is shaped like a lion holding the Eltz coat of arms in his right paw. The lion's eyes move left and right in tune with the seconds. His tail moves every quarter of an hour and he sticks out his tongue on the hour.

The fifth display case holds a collection of glass. At the top are glasses with and without lids that were owned by Elector Philipp Karl. The glasses below bear the coats of arms of other electors. The sixth display case against the window wall finally contains a colourful collection of small artefacts, including a vast array of objects and curiosities such as amulets and figures. A tiny ivory figure, for example, represents a "Dukatenscheißer" ("a man shitting gold ducats"). It was carved in Amsterdam around 1650 and is an example of the level of humour in art at that time. A round knob of a walking stick with four faces representing the Four Temperaments is also carved out of ivory.

A box contains a small collection of relics, and below it are several tobacco boxes and a card game.

In the centre of the hall, nearly opposite this small cabinet of curiosities is a tall display case with porcelain. The Hoechst porcelain manufacture, the emblem of which was the wheel of the Mainz coat of arms, began as a private company before the Mainz Elector turned it into a public limited company in 1766. Counts Hugo Franz Karl and Anselm Casimir zu Eltz were among the founding shareholders. Even though the quality of the products was high, the company was unsuccessful. The shareholders had to be paid out in porcelain, which is why the Eltz family owns so many pieces of Hoechst porcelain.

Two genealogical tables hanging between the porcelain vitrine and the mentioned silver statue of St. John Nepomuk were commissioned by Johann Jakob zu Eltz-Kempenich –

Duelling pistols with accessories made in the Kuchenreuter workshop in Regensburg

The tall display cases along the windowless wall of the large hall contain a collection of 17th and 18th-century guns displayed against a green background. There are also five pairs of pistols, the left of which was owned by Elector Philipp Karl zu Eltz. He also owned the gun hanging above these pistols. Above Philipp Karl's gun hangs an old airgun, a rarity. The firearm was made in the Walster workshop in Saarbrücken and was fired with pressurised air, making hardly any noise. The flintlock has a purely decorative function. As poachers liked to use this type of silent gun, the ordinary population was soon banned from using it. A short rhyme inscribed on the butt cap describes the feared technique: *"Paled by the power of my breath, everything within one hundred paces stumbles and falls."* The two weapons hanging on the far right of the display case are also unusual. The third and fourth guns from the top are hunting weapons. They have only one firing mechanism, but two barrels. The barrel could be swivelled after firing the first shot and was ready for a second shot.

the father of the later Elector Philipp Karl – around 1663 and are painted in oil. The panel facing the windows shows Johann Jakob sitting beneath a tree in his suit of armour. One can even recognise Eltz Castle in the picturesque landscape behind him – it is the oldest known depiction of the castle (figs. p. 3 and p. 29). The ancestors listed in the genealogical table go back to the 12th century. The second table lists the ancestors of Johann Jakob's wife Maria Antonetta Schenkin von Schmittburg.

The table display cases below the two genealogical tables contain an array of hunting weapons. The vitrine facing the windows contains, amongst other items, a wheellock with oriental style mother-of-pearl inlays, which was made around 1620 and used for shooting birds. There are also two ivory powder horns with Indian motifs, a hunting dagger and cutlery. A collection of pistols is displayed in the opposite vitrine. The 14 pistols, some of which are beautifully decorated with silver, date from the 18th century. They are grouped around a box containing two small beautifully crafted duelling pistols with all the necessary accessories. This set was made in the Regensburg Kuchenreuther workshop.

Collector's cup with a picture of Eltz Castle

Vukovar

The second room following the large hall is determined by a light, medieval groin vault resting on a mighty central pillar. The exhibition here focuses on the former Eltz estate in Vukovar. The family's links with Croatia go back to 1736, when Elector Philipp Karl zu Eltz bought the dominion of Vukovar for 175 000 Rhenish Guilders (cf. p. 28). The dominion comprised not only Vukovar itself, but also 22 villages and 15 farms with a population of about 30 000. The distant dominion was very profitable at first, but it was soon threatened by marauding troops and robbers. The landlord's obligations – such as the organisation and administration of schools, law courts and the health system as well as the construction and maintenance of bridges and roads – often cost more than what the population paid him in tithe. After the Eltz-Kempenich line moved its permanent resi-

dence to Vukovar in the late 18th century, the estate expanded following the liberation of the peasants in 1848. While the estate was now reduced by one third, the landlord's former financial obligations no longer applied. Large-scale drainage measures and the introduction of new methods of farming and livestock breeding in the second half of the 19th century turned the estate into a model farm. This was owed primarily to the efforts of Count Karl zu Eltz, who also had Eltz Castle extensively renovated at the same time (cf. p. 30). His descendents resided in Eltz Palace in Vukovar until 1944, when the Communist regime expropriated the entire estate without compensation. The head of the family, Jakob Count zu Eltz was only able to return to his home country in 1990 after Croatia gained independence; he became a member of the Croatian parliament in Zagreb. Like the town of Vukovar, Eltz Palace, too, was completely destroyed in 1991 by the Serbs.

Memorabilia from Eltz Palace in Vukovar

standing next to the table wears the uniform of the Pandours, the soldiers employed by Croatian landlords to fend off Turkish raids and for their personal protection. The maid wears a Croatian farmer's Sunday dress. A collection of 18th and 19th-century glasses can be seen in the display case on the left. The portraits in the background show Count Karl zu Eltz and his wife Ludwine, nee Pejacsevich de Veröcze.

The Armoury

A narrow spiral staircase leads down from the large hall to the lower floors of the treasure vault. The first cellar room is determined by a massive oak beam ceiling that is more than 500 years old. The wooden ceiling here, unlike in the first room of the treasure vault, is unplastered and so low that some tall visitors may have to stoop beneath the crossbeam in order to see the collection of weapons displayed in the vitrines.

A display case in the right corner contains several maces grouped around a brown-red leather shield, a so-called targe, the light shield used by bowmen. Below are two unusual combination weapons: they are pistols that could also be used as hatchets. Several bullet containers and gunpowder bottles can be seen at the bottom right.

16th and 17th-century swords, epées and daggers are shown between the windows on the rear wall of the armoury. In the centre hangs a piece of a horse's suit of armour – easily recognisable by its shape. Below are a beautifully decorated bridle, spurs and stirrups.

The corner vitrine contains a collection of hunting crossbows. The upper ones are beautifully decorated with ivory inlay and mostly date from the 16th century. The two winches were used to draw the string, as the tension of the steel crossbow was too great for the string to be drawn by hand. Depending on the type of bolt, these crossbows had a range of up to 500

The few pieces that could be salvaged from Vukovar in 1944 are today exhibited in the second room of the treasure vault.

The display cases along the right wall contain porcelain made by different manufactures, which was used by the Eltz family in Vukovar. It includes a five-piece chocolate service at the top left of the first vitrine. The small colourful cups in the centre are early 19th-century mocha cups. Most original are two collector's cups with images of Eltz Castle on the cups as well as the saucers. The candle holders were made of gold-plated bronze in the 19th century. The rear display case contains porcelain decorated with a blue floral pattern, which was made in Vienna around 1810. A table on the left of the room is set as it could have been in Eltz Palace in Vukovar. Furniture, carpet, chandelier, cutlery and crockery, even the exhibited clothes come from Vukovar. The figure sitting at the table wears a traditional dress made out of gold brocade and the fur of a sable. The soldier metres; the arrow travelled at a speed of more than 70 metres per second. Below these are smaller crossbows made out of iron that were used for bird hunting.

A simple tool or weapon chest stands to the right of the door leading to the next room. It is made of solid wood, fitted with wrought iron straps and has a rare wooden lock. Made in the 12th or 13th century, it is the oldest surviving piece of furniture in Eltz Castle – a precursor of later, more refined chests like in the other rooms of the castle such as in the Rodendorf kitchen (cf. p. 72) or the Rübenach lower hall (cf. p. 47). To the left of the door is the most striking piece in this room, a beautifully decorated ornamented suit of armour. It is entirely different to the armour we saw in the knights hall (cf. p. 63). This armour is smaller and daintier and is decorated with elaborate gold inlays. A text inscribed on the glove describes how this

View into the lower floors of the treasure vault

Helmet of the tournament suit of armour in the armoury

suit of armour was worn by a member of the related Dahlberg family when he was knighted: *"On 3 April 1764, wearing this old Eltz-Kempenich tournament armour, Baron Franz von und zu Dahlberg, burgrave of Friedberg Castle, privy councillor to the Elector in Mainz and secular governor of Worms was knighted in the St. Bartholaei Church in Frankfurt am Main by the Roman King Josepho II, who was elected on 27 March and crowned on 3 April."*

16th and 17th-century swords

The Gold and Silver Chamber

The sparkle of gold shimmers through the doorway leading from the armoury into this small chamber. The smallest room in the treasure vault is like a strong room, with treasure after treasure displayed on red velvet.

On the left is a large, ornamental bowl with a depiction of Alexander the Great, which was made around 1680 by Heinrich Mannlich in Augsburg. Ornamental bowls like this one came up in the second half of the 17th century. They have their origins in traditional washing utensils consisting of a flat washbasin and a water jug. Around 1650 silversmiths in Augsburg – then one of the most important centres for silver and goldsmiths – removed the round depression for holding the jug from the centre of the basin in order to have more room for artistic ornamentation. The washbasin thus became a beautifully decorated stately platter. As these bowls usually stood on ledges or on high shelves and were never looked at closely, the craftsmanship is usually not very refined. The bowl in Eltz Castle is an exception as it is beautifully hammered, incised and partly gilded. The scene in the centre depicts Alexander the Great after capturing the mother, wife and daughter of the besieged Persian King Dareios III in the Battle of Issus. He shows a truly noble behaviour by treating them not as prisoners but as queens. This central scene is surrounded by several smaller images along the edge of the bowl depicting scenes related to hunting, fishing and farming.

Several 17th-century wine vessels in the form of equestrian statues in front of the bowl come from Augsburg. They are made of hammered and partly gilded silver. Further to the right are a carved wooden figure out of boxwood with a silver-plated base (1650) and a tiny Flemish ivory miniature of St. George that was made around 1420 and later given a false Dürer monogramme. Next are an East German 17th-century amber tankard and several ivory beakers decorated with hunting scenes and a variety of antique motifs. An ivory relief depict-

Beautifully ornamented suit of armour, around 1520

ing a boar hunt is displayed in a black frame. Further down is a small ivory box carved with allegories of death and life. The silver bowl next to this, a credence, is beautifully decorated with enamel and an intricate floral arrangement. Further to the right are a number of equestrian figures made out of partly gilded silver. One of these 17th-century riders is the Swedish King Gustav Adolf. Two decorative antique bronze plates in 18th-century frames hang above these figures.

To the right of these is an interesting group of ten cups, which belonged to the family of Hans Anton zu Eltz and his wife Anna von Metzenhausen. They had one cup made for each of their children, each engraved with the name and birth date: Johann Friedrich 1632, Anna Maria 1634, Johann Jakob 1636, Franz Anton 1638, Karl Heinrich 1639, Johann Philipp 1641,

Hugo Emmerich 1643, Maria Elisabeth 1645, Philipp Ferdinand 1647 and Johann Anton 1649.

Further to the right is a tankard in the form of a windmill, which was used for a drinking game: the drinker had to blow through a small pipe to turn the sails of the windmill. He then had to finish his glass before the windmill stopped turning. To the right of this is a cup with a lid made in Nuremberg by the famous silversmith Hans Petzold around 1610. Below are more vessels, including a Roman clay vessel and, to the right, a beaker shaped like a swan made out of a nautilus shell as early as 1560 in Mainz.

The doors are flanked by two large twelve-armed candelabra with twisted columns crafted in Augsburg around 1630. They are made of silver with some gold-plating and crowned by beautifully crafted silver flower arrangements.

Amber tankard, 17th century

Cups of the family of Hans Anton zu Eltz

The Diana Vault

Another small staircase leads down to the last room of the treasure vault, the lowest cellar in the entire castle. The windowless room with its white barrel vault and the raw slate rock on the rear wall is plain and undecorated, while the exhibits presented here are all the more precious. To the right of the entrance is a tall display case containing sacred objects, including some of the oldest artworks of Eltz Castle. They include an aspersorium made of brass around 1150 and a round Gothic censer of around 1200. Below are four chalices, three of which belonged to the main lines of the House of Eltz, the families Eltz-Rübenach, Eltz-Rodendorf and Eltz-Kempenich. A Rhenish monstrance dating from around 1370 is made of gilded silver with enamel ornamentation (fig. p. 90). The shape is reminiscent of a Gothic church with its typical tracery and slender pier buttresses. The monstrance is crowned by a pointed turret

with a tiny figure inside. It is St. George, the patron saint of the Christian knights. A 15th-century Gothic reliquary – top left of the vitrine – looks like a small tower with a slate-decked, hexagonal roof over a cylindrical rock crystal. It is made of hammered, gilded copper. Several pieces of a Crucifixion group are displayed between the reliquary and the monstrance. The small figures depict Mary, St. John and two floating angels, all made around 1430 out of gilded silver.

The table display cases along the left side of the room contain coins, jewellery and a number of other items. On the left is a sword sheath, richly decorated with precious stones, and a belt with a colourful Roman cameo ornamented with diamonds, emeralds and sapphires. It depicts the profile of a noble Roman lady wearing a (more recent) – real – necklace. Taking a closer look at the portraits in the second room of the treasure vault, the visitor will recognise the belt – it is worn by Karl Count

Rhenish monstrance, around 1370

zu Eltz in one of the paintings. There are further a clasp as well as several broaches. Many of these items are strikingly colourful and elaborate – it is hard to believe today that they were worn only by men. The central table display case contains more precious clasps, two 18th-century belts decorated with turquoise and mother-of-pearl and a Hungarian scimitar to match it. The right table display case contains numerous coins and medals formerly owned by the electors Jakob III and Philipp Karl zu Eltz, an 18th-century purificator embroidered with gold threads and on the right a number of treasurer's keys of the 17th and 18th century. These keys have no real function, but were merely status symbols that were given to the treasurers as a sign of their power.

Other exhibits in the rear part of the room are drinking vessels in different shapes and sizes. Precious items like these would not have been in every-day use on Eltz Castle, of course. Plain ceramic or wooden vessels were used during the 15th and 16th century, while ornamented drinking vessels were reserved for special occasions such as festivities or the arrival of important visitors. On these occasions they were like a status symbol showing the host's rank and wealth. A tall display case to the left of the rock wall contains three precious wine vessels formed like ships. These "table-ships" have adorned royal tables since the 14th century. An illustration in a manuscript of the time shows the French King Charles V hosting the German Emperor Charles IV in his palace in Paris in 1378. Three such "drinking ships" have been placed in front of the guest of honour. The ships in the Eltz treasure vault are slightly younger. They were made in the 16th and 17th century and are worked in meticulous detail. The ship on the left, made in 1580, for example, which belonged to Elector Jakob III zu Eltz, even has incised ship's planks. A lansquenet stands at the hull of the ship with his shield and halberd, a jester holding a vessel and the anchor stands at the stern. The mast has a crow's nest, two

'Table ship' owned by Elector Jakob III zu Eltz, around 1580

Coconut cup in the form of a monster, around 1590

silver ribbed sails and a flag with an enamelled coat of arms at the top. The ropes attached to the crow's nest are made of twisted silver wire. A tiny figure can just be made out in the crow's nest.

The figures above the table ships are Hercules, Chronos and Atlas holding globes representing the earth, the sky and the planets. They were manufactured in Augsburg in 1685 and may have decorated the top of a large clock.

The display cases along of the stone wall contain three of the most unusual artworks in the treasure vault. On the right is a humorous drinking vessel of 1557 with two allegorical figures. One is a fat man sitting in a wheelbarrow that is being pushed by Bacchus stuck inside a vat. They represent two mortal sins, gluttony being conveyed by drunkenness. This rare work was made in Nuremberg out of cast silver and then gilded. There is only one other work similar to this one, namely that in the Grünes Gewölbe in the State Art Collections in Dresden.

The coconut cup in the form of a monster was also a drinking vessel. It was made in 1590

Drinking game with the hunting goddess Diana riding a stag, around 1600

by Caspar Beutmüller in Nuremberg and is made out of a coconut – then an extremely rare and valuable material – mounted with gilded silver. The vessel is not only a masterpiece of 16th-century Nuremberg silversmiths; it also reflects an interest in exotic countries that was typical at the time. People were beginning to explore the distant continents Africa, Asia and America, and were fascinated with their nature and culture. There was only little information available about these distant places and real artefacts or other objects were very rare. Rarities such as ostrich eggs or coconuts were extremely expensive and therefore used only for precious, elaborately worked artworks. The coconut cup in the Eltz treasure vault is an example of a beautiful combination of the exotic material with a similarly exotic motif. It represents an animal, not unlike a monster, half dragon and half wild boar. In the imagination of 16th-century artists – like the goldsmith Caspar Beutmüller – distant continents were populated by such alien and rather scary creatures.

The third display case on the left finally contains the most beautiful piece in the treasure vault. This drinking vessel depicting Diana, the goddess of hunting, riding a stag (fig. p. 93) must have been the highlight of any table decoration. The goddess's hounds as well as small frogs, lizards and insects crowd the ground beneath the stag. This vessel was more than merely a cup – it was used in a drinking game. The ornamented base conceals a mechanism that could be wound up to let Diana move along the table. When she stopped, the nearest person had to empty the entire cup. The game was made even more interesting by making the gentleman drink from the stag and the lady from the dog, both of which were linked with a short chain. This drinking game was made in Augsburg around 1600 by Joachim Fries.

Another stair takes visitors three storeys up from the lowest vault to the exit on the ground floor. This long stair originally served as a slide for the vats of wine stored in the vaults. It leads through the 4-metre outer wall of Rübenach House back into the passage to the inner courtyard.

Selected Literature

Ausonius, Mosella, edited and presented in a metric translation by Bertold K. Weis, Darmstadt 1989.

Baedeker, Karl, Die Rheinlande, Leipzig 1895. Bornheim, Werner, Rheinische Höhenburgen, Neuss 1964.

Clemen, Paul (ed.), Die Kunstdenkmäler der Rheinprovinz, vol. 17.2. Die Kunstdenkmäler des Kreises Mayen, Düsseldorf 1943.

Conzemius, Victor, Jakob III von Eltz, Erzbischof von Trier, 1567–1681: Ein Kurfürst im Zeitalter der Gegenreformation, Wiesbaden 1956.

Dehio, Georg, Handbuch der deutschen Kunstdenkmäler. Rheinland-Pfalz – Saarland, 2nd ed., Munich/Berlin 1984.

Duchardt, Heinz, Philipp Karl von Eltz, Kurfürst von Mainz, Erzkanzler des Reiches (1732–1743), Mainz 1969.

Erwein zu Eltz, Johanna, Die Burg Eltz, Frankfurt 1931.

Hotz, Walter, Kleine Kunstgeschichte der deutschen Burg, Darmstadt 1965.

Hugo, Victor, Choses vues 1848–1869, Paris 1972. English translation of the passages quoted on pages 32–34 by Kerstin Hall.

Knackfuß, Eduard, Mein Weg zur Klosterpforte, Vechta 1932.

Macquoid, Katharine, In the Volcanic Eifel, London 1896.

Powell, Cecilia, William Turner in Deutschland, Munich 1995.

Roth, F.W.E., Geschichte der Herren und Grafen zu Eltz, 2 vols., Mainz 1889–90.

Schreiber, A.W., The Traveller's Guide down the Rhine, London 1818.

Seddon, John P., Rambles in the Rhine Provinces, London 1868.

Werder, Hans (= Anna von Bonin), Im Burgfrieden, 3rd ed., Berlin 1911.

Zeune, Joachim. Burgen: Symbole der Macht, Regensburg 1996.

Practical Information

Eltz Castle is open to the public from 1 April to 1 November. Guided tours take place daily at regular intervals from 9.30 to 17.30. The treasure vault is open from 9.30 to 17.30.

There are several parking lots in the vicinity of Eltz Castle. The parking lot at the Antonius Chapel, which is reached from Münstermaifeld and Wierschen, is only 800 metres from the castle. Visitors unable to walk long distances should park here as there is a shuttle bus from this parking lot – and only from here – directly to the main gate of the castle. Other parking lots are further away, allowing visitors to approach the castle on foot along beautiful hiking paths. Visitors can drive from Moselkern to the Ringelsteiner Mühle. From there a footpath leads through the Elz valley to the castle. The walk takes approximately 40 minutes. The path from the parking lot at the Österhof near Müden is shorter, but has very steep and difficult sections. The approach from Karden takes much longer. The hike takes nearly two hours, but offers several beautiful viewing points.

Further information is available on the comprehensive website **www.burg-eltz.de**.

Burg Eltz

D-56294 Münstermaifeld

Tel.:   + 49 (0)2672/95 05 00
Fax: + 49 (0)2672/950 50 50

Internet: www.burg-eltz.de
Email: kastellanei@burg-eltz.de